Praying the Psalms

Praying the Psalms is translated from the French published by
Éditions Olivétan as *Prions les Psaums*

In the same collection of translations:

The Silence of God during the Passion
Repentance—Good News!
Spiritual Maladies
The Tenderness of God
Becoming a Disciple
From Darkness to Light

Praying the Psalms

Daniel Bourguet

Foreword by Bob Ekblad

Translated from the French

CASCADE *Books* • Eugene, Oregon

PRAYING THE PSALMS

English translation Copyright © 2016 Wipf and Stock Publishers. All rights reserved. Except for brief quotations in critical publications or reviews, no part of this book may be reproduced in any manner without prior written permission from the publisher. Write: Permissions, Wipf and Stock Publishers, 199 W. 8th Ave., Suite 3, Eugene, OR 97401.

Translated from the original French edition.
Copyright © 2000 Éditions Olivétan, Lyon, France.

Cascade Books
An Imprint of Wipf and Stock Publishers
199 W. 8th Ave., Suite 3
Eugene, OR 97401

www.wipfandstock.com

PAPERBACK ISBN: 978-1-4982-8176-8
HARDCOVER ISBN: 978-1-4982-8178-2
EBOOK ISBN: 978-1-4982-8177-5

Cataloguing-in-Publication data:

Name: Bourguet, Daniel.

Title: Praying the Psalms / Daniel Bourguet.

Description: Eugene, OR: Cascade Books

Identifiers: ISBN 978-1-4982-8176-8 (paperback) | ISBN 978-1-4982-8178-2 (hardcover) | 978-1-4982-8177-5 (ebook)

Subjects: LCSH: Bible. O.T. Psalms—Criticism, interpretation, etc. | Bible. O.T. Psalms—Devotional use. | Prayer—Biblical Teaching. | Title.

Classification: BS1433 B60 2016 (print) | BS1433 (ebook)

Manufactured in the U.S.A.   07/12/16

Contents

Translator's Note

IN SOME INSTANCES THERE are idioms in French that are difficult to translate, but that has not generally been the case with this book. There is, however, one fundamental little problem at the outset of the book. The author tells us that *La prière, c'est la beauté de l'homme*, literally "Prayer is the beauty of man"; "splendor" has been preferred to "beauty" in translation, but there is another problem to do with the generic use of "man," which is more acceptable in French than English; various shifts have been adopted to try to make the language more gender inclusive. The author's original notes and references are all to French works or translations, and it has not always been possible to provide equivalent references in English. It might also be noted that throughout the French text Psalms is referred to as the "Psalter"; this word has been used occasionally in translation, as well as "The book of Psalms." Further to the author's original notes some translator's notes have been added as footnotes, generally as glosses of the French, sometimes of a more explanatory nature; in every instance these notes have been checked with the author. Biblical passages are mostly the translator's version of the French since at times the point would be lost if this were not so; the author chooses freely among French translations.

Foreword

THE PUBLICATION OF DANIEL Bourguet's books in English is a valuable contribution to the literature of contemplative theology and spirituality that will nourish and inspire the faith of all who read them. Daniel Bourguet, a French Protestant pastor and theologian of the Huguenot tradition, lives as a monk in the mountainous Cévennes region in the South of France. There at his hermitage near Saint-Jean-du-Gard, Daniel maintains a daily rhythm of prayer, worship, Scripture reading, theological reflection, and spiritual accompaniment. All of his books flow out of a life steeped in love of God, Scripture, and the seekers who come to him for spiritual support.

I first met Daniel Bourguet in 1988 when my wife, Gracie, and I moved from rural Central America to study theology at the Institut Protestant de Théologie (IPT), where he taught Old Testament. The IPT is the Église protestante unie de France's[1] denominational graduate school in Montpellier, France.

Prior to our move to France while ministering among impoverished farmers in Honduras in the 1980s, we had come across the writings of Swiss theologian Wilhelm Vischer and French theologian Daniel Lys by way of footnotes in Jacques Ellul's inspiring books. Vischer had written a three-volume work entitled *The Witness of the Old Testament to Christ*, of which only volume 1 is translated into English.[2]

1. Then the Église réformée de France.
2. Wilhelm Vischer, *The Witness of the Old Testament to Christ*, vol. 1, *The*

vii

That book, along with a number of articles and Daniel Lys' brilliant *The Meaning of the Old Testament,*[3] exposed us to a community of Bible scholars who articulated a continuity between the Old and New Testaments that was highly relevant then and now. This connection would ultimately lead me to Bourguet.

We experienced firsthand how a literal reading of the Old Testament in isolation from the New Testament confession that Jesus is both Lord and Christ (Messiah) brings great confusion, division, and even destruction. In rural Honduras churches often distinguish themselves by selective observance of Old Testament laws and use certain Old Testament stories to inspire fear of God as punishing judge. In North America Christians were drawing from the Old Testament to justify the death penalty and US military intervention in Central America and beyond.

Wilhelm Vischer himself had been an active resister of Nazism from his Old Testament teaching post inside Germany. He resisted the misuse of Scripture to justify anti-Semitism, nationalism, and war, insisting on the importance of the Old Testament for Christian faith at a time when it was being dismissed. He was consequently one of the first professors of theology to be pressured to leave his post and eventually depart Nazi Germany before World War II, and served as Karl Barth's pastor in Basel after he too left Germany. After the war, the church in France, having been widely engaged in resistance to Nazism and deeply encouraged by Barth, invited Vischer to be the professor of Old Testament at the IPT in Montpellier.

Ellul, Vischer, Lys and other French theologians were offering deep biblical reflection that led us to look into theological study in France.[4] We wrote the IPT about their graduate program and discov-

Pentateuch, trans. A. B. Crabtree (London: Lutterworth, 1949).

3. Daniel Lys, *The Meaning of the Old Testament* (Nashville: Abingdon, 1967).

4. We were able to study with pastor and New Testament professor Michel Bouttier, who was also trained by Vischer and published broadly, including a commentary on Ephesians and a number of collections of provocative articles. Elian Cuvillier followed Michel Bouttier and is currently Professor of New Testament at

ered that Vischer had long since retired after training several generations of pastors. His protégée, Daniel Lys, had recently retired but was still available. In Lys' place was his doctoral student Daniel Bourguet, who also had been trained by Vischer. The IPT welcomed us with a generous scholarship and we were soon making plans to learn French and move to Montpellier.

We were eager for help to understand Scripture after being immersed in Bible studies with impoverished farmers in war-torn Honduras. Disillusioned with America after being engaged in resisting US policy in Central America, we felt drawn to reflect from a different context. We reasoned that studying in a Protestant seminary with a history of persecution in a majority Catholic context would prove valuable. We left Tierra Nueva in the hands of local Honduran leaders and moved to Montpellier two months early to study French and began classes in September 1988.

Daniel Bourguet taught us Hebrew and Old Testament in ways that made the language and text come alive. He invited students into his passion and curiosity as we pondered both familiar and difficult passages of Scripture. I remember continually being surprised at how seriously Daniel took every textual critical variant, even seemingly irrelevant ones. He masterfully invited and guided us to both scrutinize and contemplate each variant in its original language until we understood the angle from which ancient interpreters had viewed the text. Daniel modeled an honoring of distinct perspectives as we studied the history of interpretation of each passage. He sought to hold diverse perspectives together whenever possible, yet only embraced what the text actually permitted, exemplifying fine-tuned discernment that inspired us.

Daniel's thorough approach meant he would only take us through a chapter or two per semester. This meant we took entire courses on Genesis 1-2:4, on Abraham's call in Genesis 12:1 4, and on Jeremiah 31, Exodus 1-2, Psalms 1-2 and others. In each of his courses he

the IPT, writing many high quality books and articles.

included relevant rabbinic exegesis, New Testament use of the Old Testament, and the church fathers' interpretations. Daniel imparted his confidence that God speaks good news now as he accompanied us in our reading, making our hearts burn like those of the disciples on the road to Emmaus—and inspiring us to want to do this with others. In alignment with Vischer and Lys he demonstrated through detailed exegesis of Old Testament texts how God's most total revelation in Jesus both fulfills and explains these Scriptures, making them come alive through the Holy Spirit in our lives and diverse contexts.

While living in France every summer Gracie and I traveled from France to Honduras, spending several weeks sharing our learning with Tierra Nueva's Honduran leadership and leading Bible studies in rural villages before returning back for classes in the Fall. We had pursued studies in France with the vision of bringing the best scholarship to the service of the least in a deliberate effort to bridge the divide between the academy and the poor. Our experience of the rare blend of scholarship and pastoral sensitivity, which you will see for yourself in his books, contributed to us feeling called back to the church, into ordained ministry and back to the United States to teach and minister there. I benefited from his being my dissertation supervisor as I continued to integrate regular study into our ministry of accompanying immigrants and inmates as we launched Tierra Nueva in Washington State.

Daniel Bourguet's writings are like high-quality wine extracted from vineyards planted in challenged soil. Born in 1946 in Aumessas, a small village in the Cévennes region of France, Daniel Bourguet grew up in the heartland of Huguenot Protestantism, which issued from the Reformation in the sixteenth century. He pursued studies of theology at the IPT in Montpellier, including study in Germany, Switzerland and at the Ecole Biblique in Jerusalem. In lieu of military service, Daniel served as a teacher in Madagascar. He was ordained as a pastor in the Église réformée de France in 1972, serving parishes from 1973 to 1987. Daniel wrote his doctoral dissertation[5] while serving as

5. See Daniel Bourguet, *Des métaphores de Jérémie*, Paris : J. Gabalda, 1987.

a full-time parish pastor—a common practice in minority Protestant France, where teaching positions are scarce and pastors are in high demand. This practice often proves fruitful for ordinary Christians and theologians alike, deepening reflection and anchoring theologians in the church and world.

During our residential studies in Montpellier from 1988 to 1991, Gracie and I witnessed Daniel's interest in the early monastics and fathers of the Eastern church. In 1991 Daniel became prior of La Fraternité Spirituelle des Veilleurs (Spiritual Fraternity of the Watchpersons) and felt called to be a full-time monk, leaving the IPT in 1995 for a year in a Cistercian monastery in Lyon before moving to his current site in Les Cévennes in 1996.

Joy, simplicity, and mercy are the three pillars of Les Veilleurs, an association of laypeople and pastors founded by French Reformed pastor Wilfred Monod in 1923 (with a Francophone membership of four hundred in 2013). Members of this fellowship commit to pursuing daily rhythms of prayer and Scripture reading, including noontime recitation of the Beatitudes, Friday meditation on the cross, regular engagement with a faith community on Sundays, and spiritual retreats and reading that benefits from universal devotional and monastic practices. Les Veilleurs has served to nourish renewal in France and influenced the founding of communities such as Taizé. Under Daniel Bourguet's leadership Les Veilleurs thrived. As a member of Les Veilleurs I attended many of his annual retreats, witnessing and experiencing the vitality of this movement firsthand.

Daniel Bourguet's teaching and writing since his departure from his professorship at the IPT in 1995 have focused primarily on equipping ordinary Christians to grow spiritually through engaging in devotional practices such as prayer, Scripture reading and contemplation. Other works that will hopefully appear in English include reflections on asceticism, silence, daily prayer and the trinity. All but three of Daniel's twenty-five or so books are based on his spiritual retreats offered to pastors and retreatants with Les Veilleurs. He has offered retreats to

Roman Catholic, Orthodox, and Protestant communities throughout France and Francophone Europe and is widely read and appreciated as a theologian who bridges divergent worlds and nourishes faithful Christian practice in France. Daniel Bourguet made his first and only visit to the United States in 2005, offering a spiritual retreat in Washington State. He accompanied me to Honduras on that same trip just after Hurricane Katrina ravaged the country, teaching Tierra Nueva's leaders and accompanying me as I led Bible studies and ministered in rural communities.

Daniel left his role as prior in 2012 and now continues his daily offices, receives many seekers for personal retreats, and offers occasional retreats where he lives and writes. In alignment with the early monastic commitment to manual labor, Daniel weaves black and white wool tapestries of illustrations of Biblical stories done by pastor and painter Henri Lindegaard. Daniel's unique contribution includes his Trinitarian approach to biblical interpretation wherein he reads Scripture informed by the early church fathers, with special sensitivity to how texts bear witness directly but also indirectly to Jesus, the Father and the Holy Spirit.

Daniel Bourguet models an approach to Scripture and spirituality desperately needed in our times. He reads the Bible with great confidence in God's goodness, discovering through careful reading, prayer, and contemplation insights that feed faith and inspire practice. Daniel's deliberate reading in communion with the church fathers brings the wisdom of the ages to nourish the body of Christ today. His tender love for people who come to him for spiritual support, and the larger church and world inform every page of his writing, inspiring like practice. May you find in this book refreshment, strength, and inspiration for your journey as you are drawn into deeper encounters with God.

Bob Ekblad

Mount Vernon, WA
July 7, 2016

Preface

THIS BOOK REPRISES STUDIES given in the course of a retreat conducted at Belloc in October 1997 for the Fraternité Spirituelle des
Veilleurs. In retreats, as with preaching, bibliographic references are
left to one side; they might have had a place in marginal notes, but I
have preferred to keep them to a minimum in order to stay close to the
style of a retreat, as if the reader had also been invited to take part in a
retreat through this book.

The people present at these retreats were believers, Christians,
and the reader will see that my remarks assume this. Nothing has been
changed here, so a reader who is not a believer will undoubtedly feel
uncomfortable at times; for the host of questions that will arise for
such a reader I ask pardon; however, to go on a retreat is to retire from
the world for a time to be face-to-face with God, and the teaching at a
retreat is a means to that encounter; for this, a person would have to be
a believer. You need to know this before starting to read the book; I am
speaking here as if at a retreat, to a reader who is a believer.

Finally, again as if on a retreat, I have kept the elements of an
oral style. You are addressed here as a "reader friend," in the form of a
dialogue, a dialogue which doesn't propose to be more than an overture
to the most sublime of dialogues, that with God.

So there we are, my reader friend! May your dialogue with God
find something here to nourish it.

— CHAPTER 1 —

Searching for Real Prayer

BEFORE WE TURN SPECIFICALLY to the Psalms, a thought about prayer rises up in my heart: *Prayer is the splendor of human beings.*[1] I don't know who it was that said this or where, but it is an idea I wish were my own. How often the truth of it can be seen in people's faces; I long to be a reflection of it too.

Prayer Is the Splendor of Human Beings

Prayer is the splendor of men and women. I almost feel it would be better to add nothing and simply leave you, reader friend, to contemplate these words, much in the style of the ancients, who would only respond one pithy statement at a time. "Father, give us a word!" and the elder's reply would be, "*Prayer is the splendor of man . . .*" I, however, am little more than a novice, and we novices are often rather forward, so, please forgive me if am a bit more expansive!

Prayer is the splendor of men and women. O, that this were the only thing I should say in my life, not only to you, but to God; the product of grace, the overflow of a life, the fruit of a walk: "Lord, I recognize and confess before you now: prayer is the splendor of man."

Prayer is our splendor. There are so many wounded, disfigured people in the world, and this is the truth about all of us to some

1. French *la beauté du homme*; the beauty of man. *Man* generically, men, women, boys and girls individually! (Trans.)

extent—from the time shame first crossed humanity's face as we left the garden of Eden behind. Since then, it is our lot to weep over this lost splendor.

. . . a Splendor That Comes from God _____

It perhaps requires a lifetime of prayer for our prayer, as we turn towards God, to enable us to receive from him our primal splendor; it is not something which arises of itself; it is received. This splendor or beauty is internal, and for such splendor, such beauty, years of prayer are necessary, a slow remodeling in God's hands, a patient working of his breath, a long labor of internal creation.

God fashioned man with his potter's hands, but this was an external fashioning. The new man, the new woman, is fashioned from within, not with his hands like a hairdresser or beautician, but with his love, a little like the formation of a flower. The beauty of a flower grows from within, only then to be displayed to the world. With the new person it is much the same, save that our beauty is a reflection of God's. To stand before God makes one lovely, as the psalm says: "Those who look to him are radiant, their faces are not darkened or troubled" (34:6). Beauty is received from God.

Prayer is the splendor of human beings; it is our grandeur, our dignity, our deep mystery. This is because it participates in a previously unknown grace in which men and women stand before God in an astonishing face-to-face encounter, an encounter taking place in the absolute contrast of a simple and common servant with the Lord of lords in his infinite majesty. A face-to-face encounter which is not by chance, not fleeting, not unexpected or unprepared for, but daily, habitual, for the duration of a lifetime and filling that life.

Face-to-face with God! Have we realized what this means? We can never finish measuring the reach of these words: "in the presence of God . . ." God, the infinitely great, above everything, there with me!

How long it behooves us to be silent before we dare to pronounce the first word, the least word . . . !

In Prayer, the Truth Is Spoken . . .

If prayer is the splendor of human beings it is because it is a gushing spring of truth, a mysterious flowing fountain! To speak the truth is so rare, but prayer is a flow from the depths of the self, speech in which we are finally ourselves. Prayer is the birth of our deep internal truth, of our new being, the new birth Nicodemus had so much trouble understanding. The new birth comes to being in prayer.

In prayer, the truth of our very self leaps forth; the secret truth, buried like a treasure in a field; truth beyond the words we speak, which fills them and goes beyond them since no words can truly contain or enclose it; but truth which nevertheless speaks through the prayer even when the words are clumsy and inaccurate, too short or too hackneyed, too tired to say what we could never say of ourselves, the inexpressible secret of our being. Indeed, the deep-down truth emerges truly in prayer, and nowhere else as fully as in prayer, for the simple reason that this truth is spoken before God.

. . . Truth That Is Accepted by God

The birth of our inner being is accomplished in the hands of God and in no other way; it happens in prayer as we know ourselves to be received, heard, and understood by the one who acts towards us entirely with love. We finally become truthful because finally understood; finally true, without any mask, with no role to play, no reputation to defend, no opinion to conquer, because the love that receives us is more than equal to all that . . .

Prayer is the place where I am finally understood without any misunderstanding, understood even in what I don't say, finally listened

3

to in a silence which is true. How exquisite this is! Our silences are most often no more than half-silences, distracted silences; but God's silence is open, available, welcoming, affording us such attention that it is a blessing in itself, a miracle. We can only marvel at the mystery of this listening which receives our deep truth.

Prayer Is Encounter with God . . .

Finally, in prayer I can truthfully say "I," but also "you" (or "thou"),[2] in an intimacy without equal but in which there is nothing cavalier; it is both intimate and respectful, close and yet awestruck. What a mystery to address God in this way, and what a wonder.

"Thou, O Lord, and I, thy child . . ." Prayer is an encounter; not an abstract one, but face to face, in which I, in my flesh and my blood, stand before this God who is so true, so real, that one day he became flesh of our flesh and bone of our bone. More than face to face, it is heart to heart.

There is nothing unexpected or adventitious about this meeting; it has been anticipated by God since the first morning of the world, a meeting for which he created everything in heaven and earth. After creating everything and setting man as a jewel within creation's show case, God was silent. The seventh day consists solely of God's silence; he was silent, awaiting the prayer of his final creation, with the intense desire of hearing the sound of the human voice. What an astonishing silence this is of God's, a silence waiting to be filled, a setting awaiting a precious stone, a hope. The whole of creation is God's preparation for this meeting. In prayer, we bring fruition to God's intent, we fulfil his hope. Perhaps one day we will hear God murmur these simple words, "I have been waiting for you."

Prayer is the accomplishment of God's hopes; what a mystery and wonder!

2. French makes the distinction between *tu* and *vous*, the personal and the more formal. (Trans.)

If this encounter is longed for by God, surely it is by us too. Prayer indeed is written into our desires, into our thirst for God. Prayer is therefore the meeting of two sets of desire, a double accomplishment, a summit where two paths meet; God and man together reaching their goal. The goal of humanity is God, and God's goal is man.[3]

A goal, an objective, not just the chance meeting of two paths. God has been following his pathway for all eternity, and the two pathways embrace forever. Prayer is inscribed into the eternal longing of God and fulfils it eternally; prayer is therefore the bursting forth of eternity into our life.

If prayer is the splendor of human beings, it is because in it we meet with the God who is one, such that our own profound unity comes forth, a unity received from the God who is one; the unity of our being, our body, our soul, our heart, our spirit, our life-force . . . Our entire being is finally found to be unified, welcomed into the love of God, the love which arouses love in return, the giving of self.

In prayer, I am an offering to God, an offering of my being to this God who offers his silence to receive my prayer. Prayer takes place in this mutual self-giving; it becomes silent in the silence of God, a silence which fills God's silence, a silence full of God's silence: wonderment in the wonderment of God. We should not forget that God himself marvels, each day of creation unfolding in God's own sense of awe: "God saw that it was good." His wonderment grew from day to day until finally man was created. Then "God saw that it was *very* good" (Gen 1:31). God saw, pondered, and marveled, and then there came prayer to underscore this wonder. And so now too, God does more than see. He hears our prayer; he hears and marvels even more; the sound of our voice thrills him: "it is the voice of my well-beloved!" (Song 2:8).

---

3. The French says *"l'homme,"* that is, mankind generically, but it could also mean *"the* man," Jesus. (Trans.)

. . . and Amazed Communion

Prayer is wonderment within the wonderment of God, so great that we can say that we are in God; we stand before God and are in God, as God is before us and in us; in us, indeed, because in our prayer there is the breath of the Holy Spirit who prays in us, praying to the Father, and contemplating the Son. God in me, and I in him, without confusion or separation. Prayer is this place of deep communion, this moment of eternity in which we are no more than a yes within the yes of God, the emergence of love within the love of God. In prayer, time tips into eternity; eternity penetrates time and transfigures prayer.

If prayer is the splendor of human beings, it is because it immerses us in the beauty of God; the beauty of God in this prayer is the Spirit within us pondering the Son, and turning towards the Father. In prayer, both God and man shine with the same splendor, the same light, in the same joy and the same mutual tenderness. This beauty that shines in us so displays the beauty of God, that on certain saints it can be seen; the beauty of God rests on their countenance.

Indeed! But . . .

Prayer Has Its Difficulties

All that we have just said concerns "pure prayer," as the Fathers call it. Prayer like this is a gift from God, the work of God in us, but our prayer life is often very far from all this, and this causes us to suffer, a fact on which there is no need to insist. So, while it is true that our prayer may be far from what I have described, I describe it this way, nonetheless, since it is good to do so; prayer like this is not a dream; quite simply it is the goal of our journey, a goal from which we may be far distant but which from time to time we glimpse, perhaps afar off, but enough to cause us to marvel, just enough that we continue to press forward, just enough that we know it's real. Our prayers may be no more than the crumbs of pure prayer, but whoever has eaten, though it be but a few crumbs, already has a taste for the bread.

Our prayer, in terms of our daily portion, is confronted by a range of difficulties that sometimes leave us discouraged, dizzy, falling back through not knowing what to pray or what prayer really is. The difficulties which arise are many; we will take no more than a brief inventory, looking at just the more important.

The Difficult Silence of God

Often in prayer, unhappily we run up against God's silence. This silence, of which I consistently speak positively, is nevertheless often so heavy as to be painful; we feel nothing of its tenderness, and its hardness hurts; this is not the sweetness but the bitterness of silence; no longer is there joyous light but instead the intense darkness of God's silence.

Verbal Impoverishment

Often in prayer we run awkwardly into the inadequacy of words; we search in vain for words to say what we want to say; prayer is a verbal beggar, insatiably thirsty for the right word.

The Darkness of the Human Heart

Often in prayer, the words are available and flow easily enough, but we don't know what we wish to entrust to them. We run up against the darkness of our own identity, unable to determine accurately what we really are before God. Am I a son or a slave, his servant or his executioner, the well-beloved disciple reclining on his breast or Judas, for whom it would have been better not to have been born? Am I the object of his tenderness or of his anger, a drop of water lost in the sea,

7

or instead, one whose name is inscribed on the palm of his hand? What am I really? My heart is sometimes no more than a gaping hole which prayer searches in vain, desperately empty; prayer which founders on the darkness of my self.

Sometimes I have the impression that I know myself, the impression of being able to define what I am, but the impression is the fruit of a naïve illusion; my prayer speaks with a conviction which is really the reflection of illusion, a conviction of something quite false. At times I sense my misunderstanding and suffer as a result; at times I have no suspicion of the illusion and the devil must laugh with satisfaction, rubbing his hands. What could be more derisory or lamentable than such prayer? At times, I do suspect my error because I see something similar in others when I discover the way their prayer bears little relation to truth, and that, quite the reverse, it expresses an excess of self-indulgence or perhaps an excess of severity towards self. If others can do this with no intention of falsehood, but are merely mistaken, well, I am of the same stuff as them and, like them, can be the illusionist's victim. It might be that I speak quite sincerely when I pray, praying what I believe I can pray, what I ought to pray and what I have heard prayed; but I speak with other people's words. The prayer might be most beautiful, but it is not a beauty that is really my own; it is artificial and false. If prayer is the splendor of man, how laughable it is if the splendor is not mine. What could be sadder than to find this of my prayer and of myself.

If in the darkness I run up against the enigma of my own identity, perhaps more sadly still I may find the identity of God a riddle. Who is he really? At times I cry out in prayer—when he is so close! I clamor for the attention of someone who is "all ears" when it comes to me. In my prayer I may seek to touch the heart of the one who is already weeping with me! I beg for pardon from someone who has already pardoned me, compassion from one who is nothing but compassion towards me, the granting of prayer from the one who has already given! I plead for love from one who unceasingly gives it profusely! Behold the full tale of misunderstandings which make my prayer so unreasonable, so dissonant! Do I really know who this God is? What good is there in lifting my eyes up to heaven to pray when God is here, on his knees before me, ready to wash my feet? What value is there in prostrating myself in the Temple when he is outside, on Golgotha, hung upon a cross? What misunderstanding could be more profound? A disconcerting God of whom I cannot take hold! Who is this one for whom I have been searching so long? Have I understood something at least of the great power that resides in his extreme weakness, something of the folly of his wisdom, something of his love to which his anger is integral, something of his patience that is mixed with impatience? What can my prayer be if I still know nothing of the one before whom I stand and to whom I speak? What is there to it if it is spoken to a God of my invention, my imagination, who is nothing more than a falsehood, an idol? What bitter failure, how derisory it is, what infinite sadness there is to my aberrations . . . !

We will put a stop here to this parade of difficulties; there are quite enough of them already, and the more I go on with the list the greater the question grows within me, demanding release: is there anyone who knows the answers?

Who Then Can Teach Me to Pray?

Indeed, who will take me by the hand to unmask my idols? Who will tell me who God is in truth, who will tell me the truth of myself, and the words with which to speak of these truths? Who can keep me from my illusions about God and myself? Who can show me the way of prayer, the way of my own heart and the way of God's heart? Who really knows what it is to be heart to heart with God, and can teach me too to pray; today, not hundreds of years ago—who can I consult? Is there a man or woman of God on earth today, whether near or far, whose school I may join? Where is the clear-sighted saint who will take me by the hand—me, the blind? Prayer is so important that I am ready for anything.

The more I glimpse the beauty of pure prayer, the more I suffer the pain of seeing so poorly! The more I glimpse the goal of the journey, the more suffering my errancy brings!

Everything I have been saying concerns private prayer, free prayer which springs from the heart, the prayer which we Protestants know best; this is the way we express ourselves in preference to liturgical prayers or to prayers we have memorized and recite, written by others. For some of us, indeed, there is no other type of prayer than this. There is no doubt it is the most beautiful and the most difficult, springing as it does from the heart, which is why it claims much more of our attention. What I am going to say has this as its principal concern, so the intention is not to denounce personal prayer but, after sifting it thoroughly, to recover it in its purest form; but to do so we must put a finger on a new difficulty which is undoubtedly more important than the others, lying as it does at the root of them all, at their source.

A Heart That Defiles Prayer

Free prayer, personal in nature, comes from the heart, and indeed, it exactly expresses the contents of our heart; but what is to be found in the heart? To this question Jesus gives a shocking answer. Speaking one day to his questioners he said, "What comes out of the mouth is the issue of the heart," and then without prevarication added, "and this is what defiles man" (Matt 15:18)! This disconcerting affirmation speaks rather forcefully into our prayer life and troubles our thoughts; the prayer that comes out of my mouth and my heart—defiles me!

Jesus then continues, clarifying his comments: "It is from the heart that the evil thoughts come, murders, adulteries, sexual immorality, thieving, slander. These are the things that defile a person" (Matt 15:19–20).

The Fathers, in their thirst for prayer, paid careful attention to these verses; the desert Fathers in particular, as well as the authors of the *Philokalia*[4] after them. We have only to note the importance they accord these "evil thoughts," and their attention to the topic is considerable. It is the first thing mentioned by Jesus in his list of what defiles a person, as though what follows is no more than a detailing of "evil thoughts." Murder, adultery, immorality, and other base acts are well and truly, in their first state, simply evil thoughts.

If the Fathers were obsessed with the question of evil thoughts, it is because of their quest for pure prayer and because they were seeking, in order to denounce, everything that might sully it. It is not difficult to understand this! No one can pronounce God's name, if he has any impurity, without defiling it. What is to become of prayer if it can't so much as pronounce the name of the person it's addressed to?

Why should there be such a desire for purity? Simply, to be able to draw near to God. This was the Fathers' desire: to draw near to God and stand before him in prayer.

The Old Testament clearly states that the impure cannot approach God. Such a one cannot stand before him; impure prayer cannot reach God's heart. God's holiness keeps impurity at a distance, just as light keeps away darkness. What shadow could approach the sun without disintegrating along the way? What dewdrop could reach the sun's core? It's a radical impossibility; but just as radical is the calling into question of prayer by these men so thirsty for it!

This is the great difficulty of prayer that flows from an impure heart; how can it ever reach the heart of God?

Purification of the Heart

There is just one issue: how to have a pure heart. The Fathers' thirsty quest for prayer is a quest for a pure heart. "Blessed are the pure in

4. The extensive and diverse collection of writings and teachings of Eastern Orthodox faith. (Trans.)

heart . . ." This beatitude is the one which perhaps most attracts the Fathers' attention. "Blessed are the pure in heart, for they shall see God." Blessed are the pure in heart, in fact, because they can draw near to God; they can finally stand before him and pray to him knowing that their prayer reaches him.

This is the prerequisite for prayer: a pure heart. This is a vast project with a new question: who will show me the way to the purification of my heart? Who will show me this narrow way and strait gate? Who is there on earth today who will teach me?

The Old Testament gives a multitude of measures for the purification of the person, but it deals always with external purification and not with the heart. When the Old Testament tells us what is to be done after there has been contact with blood or with a corpse, this has nothing to do with the purifying of the heart. Faced with this lack, the Fathers sought in asceticism[5] a way to this cleansing.

"Woe is me, for my lips are unclean," Isaiah cries out to God (Isa 6:5). Then, since there was no ritual for the purification of the lips, a messenger of God, a seraph, came to cleanse the lips of the unclean man with fire. If a being sent from God was needed to purify the lips, what of the heart, hidden within as it is? Who could cleanse it except God himself? This is where the truth lies; it is God alone who can purify man's heart. The most intensely disciplined life can achieve nothing unless God himself does the cleansing. This is why David, in his search for a pure heart, turns to God alone. From the depths of his impurity he cries out, "Create in me a clean heart, O God!" (Ps 51:12). A clean heart requires an act of creation, and God alone creates. Man has only one part in this, and it is to ask of God, "Create in me a clean heart, O God!"

When the Fathers sought a road to heart cleansing in asceticism, they had no wish to substitute this for the action of God, but rather

---

5. By this term are to be understood the ordinary spiritual disciplines of prayer, Bible reading, etc., as practiced by every believer, as well as the rigors we might associate with the Desert Fathers. (Trans.)

that the intensity of their rigors express the intensity of their cry to God alone: "Create in me a clean heart, O God!"

This then is the prayer of the impure: "Create in me a clean heart, O God!"—but we also note that this cry, this prayer, is itself an impasse, an attempted squaring of the circle! If I ask God to purify my heart, I am asking it of him with an impure heart; but no impure prayer can be supposed to reach God!

. . . by the Grace of God

It is right here that the message of Jesus rings out with its surprising and wonderful good news, a way out of this mess. Indeed, an impure prayer cannot reach God, but nevertheless, God in his grace listens. In his incredible grace he welcomes the impure prayer! Our prayer life finally rests on nothing but the grace of God! What a wonder! God does me the grace of listening without needing to send an angel to cleanse my lips! His act of listening cleanses me . . .

Jesus tells us the same in the magnificent parable of the sinful man, the tax collector, who goes up to the Temple and stands as far as possible from the Holy of Holies, dirty as he knows himself to be, and, without so much as lifting his eyes towards heaven to plead for God's grace, says: "O God, be gracious to me, have pity on me, a sinner." God, in his grace, receives this man's prayer and meets his request. He is put right by the grace of God (Luke 18:13–14).

What then is the pathway of pure prayer? It is a pathway on which God in his grace comes to meet us and to clothe us in the best robe (Luke 15:22). No one can ever get there by his own efforts, not even by ascetic rigors, and the Fathers knew this well; they practiced their asceticism as the concrete expression of their intense desire for a pure heart and in total openness to God's grace, without which nothing is possible. If I have understood the Fathers correctly, asceticism is both a total stretching after God and an openness to his grace.

The quest for purity of heart is expressed in incessant supplication, on the model of that of the tax collector: "Lord Jesus Christ, Son of God, have pity on me, a sinner." There is nothing more to be said given the impure condition of our heart, nothing else to be said in our sinful condition, nothing more to say before receiving prayer in its purity from God.

Discernment in Prayer

At times we may discern the presence of impure thoughts which swirl around within us, but we quiet them so that they cannot invade our prayer. But at other times we are not so clear-sighted and we allow them to be expressed in our prayer through spiritual ignorance, like the Pharisee in the same parable who prays, carried along on the wave of his pride, "O God, I give you thanks . . ." thereby allowing these otherwise beautiful words to be soiled by the pride of those that follow (Luke 18:10–12). How often our prayers can be prideful just when we think they are humble. So many prayers are selfish, just when we think they are disinterested. The blindness of the Pharisee in the parable attracted the attention of the Fathers, who then strove to understand and discern everything of ignorant illusion at the heart of our prayers. Ascetic discipline[6] also opens us to the discernment which God alone gives in his grace.

Discernment is indispensable in the search for purity of prayer if we are to locate what we say in our prayer. Alongside wrong thoughts, our heart and our prayer also contain good thoughts (Matt 12:34–35). These are the fruit of the Holy Spirit: love, joy, peace, patience, kindness, goodness, faith, gentleness, self-control, as the apostle says (Gal 5:22), but also humility, compassion . . . All of these find their place in our prayer and in no way defile it. This fruit all comes, properly speaking, not from the heart but from the Holy Spirit, who brings

6. Again, the author is thinking in terms of ordinary spiritual disciplines, not necessarily physical rigors. (Trans.)

such thoughts to birth in the human heart, such that the true source of the thoughts and the prayer that includes them is less the heart than it is the Holy Spirit. In other terms, pure prayer comes from the Holy Spirit, which is to say from God, and goes to God.

Discernment in prayer requires particular attention because anything in us that comes from the Holy Spirit is generally very discreet, secret, hidden, humble, since the Holy Spirit is humble. This discernment is all the more indispensable because there is another spirit at work within us, an evil one; it also works in secret, not through humility, but deceit. The enemy sows, during the night, unknown to us, his tares among the wheat (Matt 13:24–30), evil thoughts in the midst of the good, false joy in the true, false peace in the true . . . And this all finds a place in our prayer! Who will teach us to discern the wheat from the tares in the field of our heart and our prayer, so that when we think to bring God wheat, there are no tares offered?

In short, we see, reader friend, how precious it is to know how to be discerning if we are to pray our best. Without this, prayer seriously risks being little more than a confused effusion of sentiment, emotional verbiage which vents everything without sifting the pure from the impure—impurity defiling what is pure . . . !

The need for discernment I am speaking of does not only concern what is to be found in our own heart, in ourselves; the same discernment is also necessary for all that concerns the work of the Holy Spirit in the heart of those for whom we are praying. What am I to ask of God for my brother if I know nothing of the secret work of God in his life? I, who have so much trouble discerning what is going on in myself, how much more trouble will I have knowing what is going on in my brother, or still more in the life of someone unknown who has asked me to pray—or even en masse for those I have never met, for whom I pray nonetheless . . . Oh! the prayer of a blind man, speaking of what he cannot see, his prayer shot through with illusions, mistakes, and ignorance . . . !

True Prayer Comes from God _____

Who then will intercede in truth? Who will confess the collective sins of the Church and of society, which no single person can even discern? Who will pray for those who have never prayed? Who will express the suffering of the abused child who doesn't know how to tell it? Who will express the prayer of the mentally ill? Who will pray for the world itself the true prayer, the one which God awaits? How poor and needy and blind is our prayer . . . !

Who knows how to pray correctly? The answer to the question is clear: the Holy Spirit! He alone knows how to pray (Rom 8:26). He alone knows how to take the groans and cries, the silences, the stammerings and sighs of creation and make of them true prayer; he alone, as one with the Son of God (Rom 8:34). The Son of God intercedes at the right hand of the Father, and his prayer is true.

The Son and the Holy Spirit pray truly to the Father; this means that the only true prayer is internal to the Trinity, spoken by God to God. Prayer gushes from the heart of the Trinity. Pure prayer is God's; unceasing prayer is God's. If I am looking for pure prayer, that's where it is found, in him, in the Trinity. Perhaps it is to be found nowhere other than in the Trinity, but it does exist, and indeed, through all eternity. Profound prayer which speaks the inexpressible things of the world, prayer which floods the world's darkness with light, prayer which envelops the entire world in infinite love, prayer from which no one is excluded, where no one is betrayed or fails to be understood: a prayer of fire which purifies and burns up the world and our heart without consuming them.

But it is also prayer which itself awakens in us the thirst for prayer; it is pure prayer which creates in us a longing for pure prayer; it is unceasing prayer which causes this longing for unceasing prayer, for prayer which makes us forget everything else to give ourselves wholly to it, and desire to be nothing but prayer. What if to be in the image of God means to be prayer as he is prayer? The Son prays, and the Spirit is in prayer before the Father, who never ceases to welcome this prayer; the more we discover in God the importance of prayer, the greater our thirst for it grows.

Only, this pure prayer is God's and not ours. We are witnesses to it, but unable to participate, to go in. We remain to one side, unable to enter, and the question returns: who will show us the way to enter Trinitarian prayer? What saint will open the door of this holy prayer to us? Who is close enough to God, and who has sufficient part in his prayer to share it with me? What person will lead me onto the bosom of the Trinity and open to me their prayer?

"I" have so many questions about prayer! "I" am prepared to scour the earth in search of a teacher and a school of prayer, but sensing beforehand it would surely be fruitless . . .

Who will teach us to pray? To this question the Bible proposes an answer that is amazing, unprecedented and wonderful:

the one who will teach us to pray is none other
than God himself . . .

CHAPTER 2

The Father Teaches Us to Pray

God Teaches Us to Pray . . . _____

HERE I AM WITH my intense thirst for real prayer and with the constant sorrow of my actual wretched prayer life. I have this insistent question: who will teach me to pray? And here is the surprising and overwhelming answer the Bible proposes: it is God himself who will teach me to pray!

I was searching for a man or woman of God, and God proposes himself! I looked for a saint, and I find one in God! Beyond all expectation, my hopes are fulfilled. The teacher I was prepared to find at the other end of the world might have been just another charlatan, a blind leader of the blind; how is a blind man to tell if his leader himself is blind? But now, God steps forward; what a wonder! I can follow him in total confidence. There is no need to travel the earth; right here and now what I need is given.

. . . by Giving Us the Psalms _____

How does God go about teaching us to pray? What is his method, how does he teach? It's not by coming to conduct a course on prayer, though he might, and we would be happy about it; no, he does much better; he demonstrates his own prayer, he gives it to us; not just one prayer, but a hundred and fifty! What he gives us is the book of Psalms, and the book of Psalms is in fact 150 prayers of God, offered to us.

In the kingdom of prayer, there are 150 entranceways; we may go in by any one of them and each time we will discover God in a different aspect, in a different light. After we have made a tour of these 150 prayers, God tells us that he has another to propose, namely, the Lord's Prayer; however, we will occupy ourselves for the time being with these 150; 150 wonderful gifts.

At the heart of the Bible, resounding with the word of God, we find the book of Psalms. In it too we hear God's word, in this instance the word as prayer.

It is found at the heart of the Bible, not at its outset, since it is best to enter prayer without being precipitate; there are obstacles to prayer which become apparent in the book of Psalms and require, as a preliminary, lengthy preparation in the form of the preceding books; these help us enter into God's history with men. With a deliberate approach we eliminate a good number of difficulties.

The Book of Psalms is in the center and not at the end of the Bible; we should not be silent too long in our relationship with the one who is causing us little by little to enter into intimacy with him.

Psalms is at the heart of the Bible, a jewel in its showcase.

The Difficulties of Prayer Dispersed

The Book of Psalms is almost the largest in the Bible, telling us the importance God accords prayer. As we follow our teacher, he will lift away the difficulties discussed in the first chapter.

You may have been held up, the teacher of prayer tells us, by the inadequacy of words to express your prayer, but here the words are given you in 150 prayers of tremendous variety.

You wanted to know yourself better so that in this way you wouldn't trip over yourself; well here in these prayers, little by little you will discover yourself in every aspect. Pray the Psalms and you will find the truth about yourself.

Are you hurt by my silence? Incline your ear and in the psalms you will hear the sound of my voice.

Are you troubled by the impurity of your heart? Let my word inhabit you; it is a fire which will purify.

Meditate the psalms, patiently, in solitude; ruminate over them; listen to them; make them your own and all will become clear. The Book of Psalms will slowly fashion your identity as a praying being. Take the time necessary; the objective makes the effort worthwhile; don't wait any longer to begin; don't be hasty, but don't delay; your very life is involved in this.

We must recognize the truth here; the obstacles encountered in our prayer life turn out all to be surmountable, one after another, thanks to God who leads us through the Psalter.

Were you looking for the words to pray? They are here! All the words for prayer are in this Book of Psalms, those of trust, of thanksgiving, of repentance, of praise, of pain, of compassion, of intercession, every facet of private prayer and also of communal.

The words of the psalms enlighten, quiet, impel us onward and cause us to discover new aspects of prayer. They often go beyond anything we know how to say or ever could say.

At times they repulse and, violent as they are, we hesitate to speak them: "O Babylon the wretched . . . Happy is he who will seize your infants and dash them against the rock!" (Ps 137:9). There are also words that we receive as being from God but they are beyond us, not because they are impure in some way, but because our heart is still unclean and has no entrance to understanding. As long as the light of God is still darkness to us, so long as our dark heart is unable to see the true light, our part is to silently wait for the cleansing of the heart, when finally the words become our own.

At times, on the other hand, they touch the hardness of our heart and cause it to say things it had never dared before. "I love you, Lord!" Until I discovered Psalm 18, I had never dared speak like that to God; "I love you, Lord!"

In sum, we find in the Book of Psalms the fullness of prayer; everything is expressed, from the purest love to the most violent invective, from the softest tenderness to the most vehement anger, from entire confidence to the most pernicious doubt . . . Plenitude and profundity, the Book of Psalms opens up to us the ways of prayer, beyond what we might glimpse, beyond all our efforts; plenitude and profundity that we could never attain alone, but which we receive from God. This is God's gift to us; a unique and astonishing gift in which man recovers his beauty.

If prayer is the splendor of human beings and we have lost this native splendor, the loss is neither irremediable nor definitive. The Book of Psalms invites us to once again take hold with confidence of the way of prayer, this pathway of God, despite our betrayals and denials, despite our disfigurements and distorted features . . . Through the psalmists' prayer, God fashions his creature anew and gives us the interior beauty which shines in our face. The Psalter is the splendor of man in 150 colors; it is the music of mankind in 150 harmonies; no other music so rich, no light so dancing with color.

The Road to God's Heart _____

The first word of the Book of Psalms is "Blessed" and the last is "Alleluia." Between these two words men and women come to creation as they practice these prayers; between the blessing and the praise of the whole universe. The last syllable of the word "Alleluia" is "ia" or "Jah," the first syllable of the name of God, as though the whole Book of Psalms leads us into the inexpressible, and trails off into silence, lost in the heart of God, beyond anything that can be said; we reach into the measureless heart of God where man's creation takes place, in eternal heart-to-heart intimacy. Man is created, both personally and together with others, in this praise which is both singular and communal, both alone before God and together with the brothers and sisters.

What am I saying? Is this a dream? Is it really the case that God can teach us to pray and fashion us through this multifaceted prayer?

Tell me, who better than God could teach us the words God awaits, the words he longs to hear from his creature? Who better than God could ever tell us our true identity, we who come from his hands? Who better than God knows the way to God's heart? Who better than the Son knows the Father's heart, and who better than the Holy Spirit knows the depths of God? This is the very God, the Trinitarian God, who takes us by the hand to teach us to pray. The way he shows us in the Book of Psalms is the way of light and of fire, even if we are still blinded by its overbearing power. We seek for a school of prayer and a teacher of light; the Book of Psalms is the school (with 150 doors) and God is the teacher.

The Book of Psalms Raises New Difficulties _____

This is wonderful, but from our first steps in this school we encounter obstacles, difficulties, enigmas, so that at times we come to a full stop right in the middle of a psalm, unable to get past this or that difficult verse. While the Psalter answers certain questions, it raises others; so we begin to search out the best way to use it. What good is the most sumptuous gift if I am unable to profit from it? I am offered a lovely sailing boat but am unable to advance so much as a stone's throw from the quay, ashamed that I don't measure up to the beauty of the gift . . .

We stand before Psalms like the Ethiopian eunuch before the book of Isaiah . . . Lord, send us a Philip who can explain what we are reading, what we are praying . . . !

Better than Philip, God himself comes to explain; God himself comes to provide the necessary instruction. This is the teacher to whom to listen, an amazing teacher, the Trinity.

> The Father comes to teach us to pray,
>
> the Son comes to teach us,
>
> the Spirit comes to teach us. . .
>
> we listen to this threefold teaching.

The Father Comes to Teach Us to Pray

As we immerse ourselves in the Book of Psalms to discover its prayers, something of a most surprising nature is often to be found. Alongside the prayers addressed to God, we frequently find words addressed to us!

> *I will instruct you, I will show you the way to go,*
>
> *I will counsel you and watch over you.*
>
> *Do not be like the horse or the mule*
>
> *Which have no understanding;*
>
> *They must be held in with the bit and the bridle,*
>
> *Or they will serve no purpose.* (Ps 32:8–9)

These are certainly not words addressed to God, but those addressed by God to us. It is we who need instruction, not him; but the verses which immediately precede these are indeed prayer spoken to God.

Here is a surprising discovery; at the very heart of the praying psalms, at times there is a word from God which interrupts the prayer, as though the teacher is interrupting his disciple to show him the right way. The Book of Psalms, then, contains at its core, instructions from God to teach us how to advance towards him; God himself comes to point out, to signpost, the way of prayer. His instructions are not provided in a preface or a separate leaflet, but at the very heart of the Psalms, right in the middle of a prayer (and Psalm 32 is not the only one to be interrupted by instruction from God!). Where we looked for a handbook on usage, we find it included, a gift within a gift.

This verifies what we have previously said; if we were over-whelmed by the silence of God, we are to incline our ear and hear his word in the Book of Psalms; here it is—"I will instruct you, I will show you the way to go . . ."

In Psalm 32, God's instruction is limited to two verses, but else-where the instructions may occupy a whole psalm. This is the case with Psalm 50, in which God presents himself to instruct his people, and above all, from verse 16, to correct them where their behavior is wrong. We go from one surprise to another; in this book of prayer where we expect instruction on prayer, instead we receive, not instructions on piety, but on ethics! The wicked man whom God corrects in 50:16–23 is interrupted in the midst of religious practices, his meditation of the Scripture ("Who are you to recite my laws and keep my covenant in your mouth?" [v. 16]), and critiqued for his moral comportment; "When you see a thief he becomes your friend, you are at home among the adulterers; you give your mouth to evil and your tongue to deceit" (vv 18–19).

The Way of Prayer Is a Way of Love

We need to submit ourselves to the evidence: the way of piety, the way of prayer, is also the way of ethics, the road of obedience to the com-mandments of God, the way of fidelity to what is summarized as the love of God and of one's neighbor. The message indeed seems to be the following: fulfil the law and you will know better how to pray. Love, and you will find in love the pathway of prayer. There is a profound osmosis between the ethical life and the life of prayer.

What a surprise: at no moment in the Book of Psalms does God give us instructions on piety, on the correct gestures with which to pray, on the forms of prayer! Everything goes back to behavior. It is truly the case: take care of your ethical life, and your prayer life will go better. The severity with which God at times gives such ethical instruction shows how essential this approach is.

For those who may not yet be convinced of this, Psalm 15 will open the eyes of the heart. In this psalm God's instructions do not interrupt the prayer but are instead stated by the one who prays:

Lord, who may dwell in your tent?

Who will live on your holy mountain?

In other words, "Who may come into your Temple to pray? Who will come before you to worship?" A person who asks questions like this is thirsty for prayer. The answer God gives him takes up the rest of the psalm, and it is entirely to do with ethics:

He who conducts himself blamelessly,

Who acts justly

And speaks the truth in his heart.

He bites his tongue,

Does no wrong to his brother,

Nor spreads rumors about his neighbor.

In his eyes a reprobate is condemned,

But he honors those who are faithful to the Lord.

If he swears to his own hurt,

He does not take back his word.

He lends money without usury,

And will take no reward against the innocent.

Whoever does this will never be shaken.

All the instructions given by God in Psalms are of this nature. Of course, God awaits our praise, but praise in harmony with love for our neighbor. The beauty of psalmody does not lie in the music but in love. How could there be any purity of prayer out of a pure heart when the heart does not know how to love? Fullness of prayer crowns fullness of love.

Why is this so? Why this pathway of ethics in order to advance in prayer? I believe the answer is clear: God is love and it is only in love that he can be met. Only love can connect with the heart of God.

The quest for pure prayer has led us to the quest for a pure heart; and it is love which purifies the heart. It is the love of God for us which purifies the heart, and, as we extend love to God and to our neighbor we keep our heart in the purity received from God. Learn, then, to love and you will know how to pray. This is the instruction the Father gives from one end of the Psalms to the other, in repeated appeals. Not just at the beginning, once and for all, but from one end to the other, because we have never finished learning what it means to love.

God Sends David as Company

This was the first point in God's teaching; he does not stop there but completes it with a second. For our instruction, God also sends us David, in whose mouth he put the psalms. He gives him to us, not as a teacher, but as a classmate, a companion who is also being led by God, one who prays alongside us.

When I say David, I mean this as an inclusive, global name, since we also have the Sons of Korah, Heman, Ethan, Solomon and the other authors of the psalms, enough indeed to fill a classroom! To simplify things I speak simply of David.

To have God as a teacher simply on his own is very good, but what a joy it is to have along with him a few companions. David is the brother God gives us, an older brother who has already gone rather further than us along the way of prayer, a brother who, like us, has questions about prayer, inquietudes, doubts, thirst; he is no superman or saint, but a neighbor who shares with us the sinful condition of mankind, a brother who we find to be so close in terms of his fragilities and limitations, a wonderful companion! God gives us a great gift in David!

It is true that David speaks what he receives and understands from God in his own words, and because, certainly, they are the words of his period, some effort is needed to grasp them; but the effort is worthwhile.

David, then, is a companion in the school of prayer, but he is also revealed as a remarkable teacher, from whom we learn a great deal. His courage in praying so that we might hear is remarkable. We become witnesses of his prayers; we witness, for example, the confession of his sins in Psalm 51; what courage and humility! It is easy enough to praise God before others, but to confess one's sins! David draws us to his side and opens his heart. It is not really we to whom he opens up, but God, yet he does it in such a way that we can learn in our turn to open our hearts before God; this can be so difficult. A wonderful brother, for sure, and a fine teacher.

David Steps Aside . . .

The danger in opening one's heart in the presence of a witness is self-display, with the pride that underlies it. We might repent with pride before others, but true humility is self-effacing. This is just what we find in David; he steps aside.

In all the psalms David effaces himself. In Psalm 51, where he confesses his sin, he never describes his fault; he says nothing of what is peculiar to him. The title of the psalm tells us the context, and we know what had happened, that David had fallen into adultery with Bathsheba, and effected the murder of her husband; but the psalm itself says nothing of the murder or the adultery; there is no detail, no display! David tells us his fault, without stating it; he says everything without pushing himself forward; this is his self-effacement, his great humility. The same happens in Ps 32:5, as in the rest of the Book of Psalms. The elements which pertain solely to David as stated in the titles of the psalms are not found in the prayers they introduce.

The attitude David adopts is very rich in instruction for us. In acting as he does, David teaches us to speak only to God and not to any third party about certain details of life, not even to the closest of brothers; no one will ever be closer to us than God; no one else has his ear so attuned as does God. David has the courage to speak before us and the delicacy[1] not to say everything. To tell everything to God purifies the heart, and delicacy avoids soiling the heart of the brother or sister. The delicacy is a way of loving and respecting. God is able to forgive, wipe away and forget what he hears. A brother may be able to forgive but not to forget what he has heard. I will be forgiven by my sister, but she will be stained and defiled to some degree. Repentance purifies my heart, and repentance in my brother's presence edifies him, but delicacy protects the brother's heart. This delicacy has to do with wisdom; whoever is growing in wisdom makes great strides along the way of prayer and helps his or her fellow do so too.

. . . and Offers Us His Prayers . . .

By removing the details of his life from his prayers, David enables us to make his prayers our own, and this is another way in which we discover David's admirable self-effacement. They are David's prayers, but, by not letting slip the details of his own life, David is able to give his prayers to us, so we can adopt them without any reservations. We can pray Psalm 51 without necessarily having been an adulterer and murderer; with this psalm we can confess the faults which are ours alone. This is wonderful self-effacement from a teacher who prays in our presence

---

1. The French here is *pudeur*. The author has a book devoted to the *pudeur* of God; it means modesty, reserve, delicacy, even a sense of shame (Trans.).

and then lets us pray afterwards without coming between us and God! He prays alongside but without getting in the way, without in any way disturbing the intimacy of heart-to-heart contact with God which we may enjoy thanks to the prayers he gives us. He is so humble that we scarcely know if the prayers are truly his. Some of the psalms are, so to speak, unsigned, and this too indicates great humility. Thanks to David we can appropriate his prayers and through them express our own experiences, not those of someone else.

. . . as He Offers Them to a Multitude of Brethren

This wonderful self-effacement of David means we discover another gift, that of a multitude of brothers and sisters. Stepping aside as he does, he presents us with all his prayers, as we have just said; equally, though, he gives them to a host of other men and women who have received them before us, who have recognized themselves in them and made them their own. When we pray the Book of Psalms, they are there with David, together with us.

We discover this host of witnesses which has been growing year by year for three thousand years, a host which has prayed and still prays these psalms in the four corners of the earth. If David is a brother, a myriad of others rise up before us; they go before us, alongside us and follow us along the way of prayer; they have entered by the 150 doors of this school where God is the sovereign teacher. All have received the Book of Psalms from God and hear the word of God sounding through it.

Among them are Jews and Christians, and perhaps others too, praying silently at the heart of this great host, in the secret place of God.

Among them are Protestants, Catholics, Orthodox, pre-Chalcedonians, Baptists, free church, Methodists, Lutherans, Reformed, new reformed . . .

Among them are Augustine, Jerome, Bernard, Luther, Calvin, as well as Abba Moses, Abba Agathon, Isaac of Nineveh, Ephraim the Syrian, John Climacus, Dorotheus of Gaza . . .

Among them are a certain unknown elderly woman from a valley in the Cevennes, a hermit from the Judean desert, a black gentleman from a Johannesburg shantytown, a political prisoner in his cell . . . young, old, wise, unlearned . . .

Such is the great host of our brothers and sisters.

Some of them have learned the Book of Psalms by heart, and recite it every day; others never get beyond a particular verse which they meditate and pray for years on end.

Some are so saturated in it that in each verse they perceive something of God's light, and in each psalm, a ray of beauty from God. Others stop in tears over some one verse which impacts them powerfully.

Some have died with a psalm on their lips, breathing out with their final gasp a word which others take up as in a relay, a new stage on the way of prayer.

Some have written commentaries to help us follow this route traced out by God, the road from which David steps out of the way to let us pass. This is the great host for whom David composed Psalm 133; "Indeed, it is good and sweet for the brothers to live together in unity!" For David too all these people are brothers, a present from God to him, as to us. Here is the truth, that it is not David who gives us these brothers, these sisters, but God. We are together on the road of prayer, together before the same difficulties, the same obstacles, united in a thirst for God, a thirst for prayer. The longer I live in solitude, the more I experience this great company of fellows along the way of prayer.

Among These Brothers Is Christ . . . _____

At the heart of this great crowd we find still more brothers; we find Matthew, Mark, Luke, John, Paul, and others. These particular brothers were so full of the psalms that they quoted them continually in their writings, more than any other book in the Old Testament. They were truly formed by the psalms; they breathe them.

Formed as they are by the Book of Psalms, they all speak of a man from Nazareth who was also soaked in the psalms to the point of being a living commentary on them. He had prayed the psalms each Sabbath in Galilee; as a child, his father and mother would have taught them to him; as a grown man, he prayed them with his disciples, all the way to the upper room in Jerusalem on the eve of his death. He shared bread and wine with the disciples, "after having sung the psalms" as we are told in Matt 26:30 and Mark 14:26, alluding to Psalms 113 through to 118.

This man made his way into the psalms to dwell in them and to be dwelt in by them, to such a degree that he died on a cross with the opening words of a psalm in his mouth and the remainder of it in his heart: "My God, my God, why have you forsaken me?"(Ps 22:1). For him to die like this, the psalms must have been fixed deep inside him.

"*Eli, Eli, lamah sabaqthani*" (Matt 27:46); when Jesus quotes from Psalm 22 it is in Aramaean and not in Hebrew. He spoke the psalm, not in the language of the priests, but that of the people; not the language of the temple, but that of the street; not that of the festivals and religious ceremonies, but of everyday life in its ordinariness. Jesus was impregnated with the Book of Psalms, not as a matter of ritual but as his breath, in communion with his people. More than a living commentary on the Psalms, Jesus is the Book of Psalms come to life, flesh, and blood.

. . . Contemplated by David as He Composed the Psalms

Where David effaces himself so humbly, it is surely to allow room for us and also for the whole crowd which was to follow him, and, above all, to give place to he who was to come after him but was before him, the one who would be anointed by God and be called the Son of God. David effaces himself before the Son, so that He might pray, to give place to Him, for Him to be our true guide along the way of prayer. David knew how to pray, but he was also aware that his son would be greater than him and would lead us right into the heart of God.

Everything just said about the self-effacement of David before Christ is not reading into the text something that isn't there, a re-reading that forces this meaning onto David. Not at all; it is something that is really present on David's lips but in a way that is so discreet as to be perceptible only beneath the surface of the psalms. David truly contemplated Christ, but this is not something we will discover unless we are ourselves involved in contemplation of Him. David saw and marveled!

An example which shows David with Christ in view is in Psalm 8, where David is in wonderment before the splendor of God: "How magnificent is your name in all the earth!" At the heart of the psalm, David makes plain the foundation on which his sense of wonderment rests: "What is man that you think on him? You have crowned him. . . put all things under his feet. . ." Undoubtedly, David here is describing a king, "crowned" by God and to whom God has put all things in subjection; according to the terminology of the period, "to put under the feet" means "to subject." But who is this king—this king other than David? Why didn't David say, "Who am *I* that you should think on *me*?" This is exactly how he expressed himself, in the first person, when Nathan came to him announcing the covenant God was making with the Davidic line. David's reaction on that occasion was as follows: "King David presented himself before the Lord and said, 'Who am I,

Lord God, and what is my house, that you should have brought me to be what I am?'" (2 Sam 7:18). Here in Psalm 8 we find something else, a quite different tone; David does not speak of himself but of another: "Who is *he*? You have crowned *him*; you have put all things under *his* feet. . ." The one he speaks of is designated at first in a very imprecise way ("Who or what is *man* or *the man* that you should think on him?"), but then in a more exact and unmistakable way: "And the *Son of man* that you should care for him?" The Son of Man! The one of whom David speaks and whom God has made king is still unnamed, a shadowy figure in the Old Testament, but David, truly, contemplated him from afar:

> You wished him to be a little lower than God:
>
> you have crowned him with glory and honor;
>
> you have established him as head over the works of your hands;
>
> you have put all things under his feet:
>
> the sheep and the cattle and even the wild beasts,
>
> the birds of the air and the fish of the sea . . .

The royalty David describes does not resemble his own; there was never any question of David having dominion over the animals. The royal nature of the one David ponders is of another type altogether. "What is he?" David exclaims, marveling as he contemplates the one he names "Son of man"; he ponders from afar the one whom the New Testament presents in full light. David points towards another, and invites us too to look past him into the beyond.

All that we have said is nothing more than what the author of the Letter to the Hebrews says too; he takes up the same verses from Psalm 8 (in Heb 2:6–9) and identifies the one before whom David marvels: the Son of Man of whom David speaks is Jesus Christ, the epistle says. From this we can understand the true nature of David's effacement; he draws back before the one he considers greater than himself, more royal, "a little lower than God."

For his part, Jesus himself was also aware of this effacement of David's before him. It is just what he said with regard to another psalm in one of his encounters with the Pharisees: "Of whom is Christ the son? 'Of David,' they replied. Very well; tell me then, why David calls him his Lord, in Psalm 110."

For Jesus, as for the Pharisees, David was speaking of Christ in this psalm. On this point Jesus was in agreement with the Pharisees and with all the Jews of his era, so this is not where the divergence in views lay; it consisted rather in the relationship envisaged between David and Christ. For the Pharisees, Christ was the Son of David. Jesus responded by opening their eyes to another aspect of things. It was enough for him to draw attention to what David himself said; in what terms had he spoken of Christ? Not as of his Son, but as his Lord. Jesus points to Psalm 110 without taking the argument any further since this was sufficient. David regarded Christ as his own Lord, and this is what Jesus underscores, to make it plain to us.

Before his Lord, David could only draw back into the shadows; this is what he does in Psalm 8, as in Psalm 110 and the rest of the Book of Psalms. The offering David makes of his prayers is certainly meant for us, but, still further, it is for this Lord whom he contemplates from afar, his Lord. It is in this offering that we see the marvelous self-effacement of David. Yes, he wished to hear the psalms in our mouths, but much more he wished to hear them in the mouth of the one he calls "the Son of Man" and "his Lord."

David knew himself to be provisional, a promise of another. As a good teacher he does not point to himself but to the one he already honored, and in whom he recognized the true spiritual master.

The psalms are both David's offering and an invitation to us to hear them in the mouth of the one to whom they are offered, Christ. In this way we are led, by David himself, straight to Christ. This is the direction we must now turn if we are to learn to pray.

— CHAPTER 3 —

The Son Teaches Us to Pray

Christ Comments on the Psalms _____

ON THE ROAD TO Emmaus, Jesus taught his disciples to read the
Scriptures: "Beginning with Moses and the prophets, he explained to them from the Scriptures the things concerning himself"
(Luke 24:27). Learning how to read the Scriptures simply means
learning to discern what they say about Christ.

What exactly is meant by "the Scriptures"? A little further in this
account, Luke is specific: "It was necessary that everything be accomplished that was written in the Law of Moses, in the prophets and in
the psalms. Then he opened their hearts that they might understand the
Scriptures. He said to them: thus it is written that Christ must suffer"
(Luke 24:44–46).

The passage is fundamental in more ways than one. First, understanding the Scriptures means understanding Christ, and more
precisely, understanding the cross ("it is written that the Christ must
suffer . . ."). Further, it is Christ himself who enables understanding
("he explained to them"); he is the teacher who "opens the heart" of his
disciples. Last, it is in the Book of Psalms in particular that we grasp
the mystery of Christ on the cross.

"He explained to them": Jesus presents himself as the commenta-
tor on the Psalms in order to reveal to his disciples "everything that
concerns himself." In this way, insomuch as we are disciples, we are

invited to reread the Psalms, there to glean everything that concerns Christ.

Jesus gives his commentary on the Book of Psalms after his death and resurrection, which is to say, at a time when the disciples still retained fresh in their memory every detail of his life. He could now make apparent to them surprising connections and correlations. He tells them how to read afresh phrases such as "they have pierced my hands and my feet" (Ps 22:17); this was something David never experienced himself—so who then was in view? "They cast lots for my clothing" (Ps 22:19). Does that remind you of anything? "They gave me vinegar to drink" (Ps 69:22). Doesn't all that you have seen begin to make sense? How amazing! And this is just the start of a way of reading that provides an unsuspected array of details which apply to Christ. In this way the Book of Psalms is illuminated, just as is the life of Christ, each shining in the light of the other.

Christ Praying the Psalms

Much more than being simply a commentary on Christ, reading the Book of Psalms reveals to those who follow him the depth to which Christ is present there. We have surely read, "They have pierced *my* hands and *my* feet"; who is speaking here? This verse does not speak of Christ, but is spoken by him; this is not David speaking but Christ. "They cast lots for *my* clothing"; we find the same thing where he says, "They have given *me* vinegar to drink," as well as in a large number of other psalms. It is amazing; to say that the Book of Psalms speaks of Christ is far short of the reality—which is, that it is Christ who speaks in the Psalms. In the light of his death and resurrection, we discover that Christ lived the Book of Psalms, that he prayed it, and that the Psalms sound much better in his mouth than in David's.

We may have felt wounded by the silence of God, but then, as we listened carefully to Psalms, we found first that we hear in them words from the Father; but now we hear the words of the Son, wonderful words!

Returning from Emmaus, the disciples said of their discovery of the Psalms, "Did not our hearts burn within us when he spoke to us along the way, as he explained the Scriptures to us?" Certainly their hearts burned; but it was not just a question of who it was that was speaking then, but that we hear him in the Psalms themselves.

On every occasion, when a disciple opens the Book of Psalms and listens closely, he hears Christ pray. If we listen really carefully, we hear what was previously unheard, all the prayers of Christ on the roads of Galilee, on the mountain, in the desert, at Gethsemane, on the cross . . . These words are the words of fire which burn in the heart of whoever hears them.

Therefore, when you open the Book of Psalms, begin in silence, be attentive, listen . . . Your heart will burn when you hear the prayers of Christ, your Lord. This is the way he will lead you along the pathways of prayer, along the pathways within God's heart. The Father is your teacher; the Son is too.

Listen First to Christ Praying the Psalms . . .

We have arrived here at an essential, primordial point. To pray a psalm we have to begin with silence; this means renouncing any attempt to appropriate it too quickly; we renounce any attempt to pray too quickly, in order first to listen to the master, Christ, as he prays it. This is an indispensable step from the moment we recognize Christ as our teacher; without this, we enter the psalms from entirely the wrong perspective, and the Psalms will remain an enigma. The greatest part of our difficulties stems from neglecting this step. We take the psalms to ourselves without listening to our teacher praying and explaining them. Who are we to put ourselves forward like this, and to not allow Christ to show us the way?

Indeed, the first thing to do is to be silent until our heart begins to burn, no matter how long it takes! A silence could never be too long if it is filled with the prayer of Christ! Blessed is he whose heart begins to burn as he meditates the Psalms, since Christ is opening his spirit. With Christ the psalms finally fall open and are illuminated with unspeakable light. Without him, the Book of Psalms will remain closed, as will our heart.

The Psalter is sealed with seven seals, but, like the apostle John, we have only to cry out until such time as Christ comes to open the seals, one by one before us. This will take just as long as it takes! At the opening of the seventh seal there will be a silence in heaven of half an hour (Rev 8:1). Half an hour! In this silence I will hear him, hear him pray . . .

. . . and Then Pray the Psalms in Christ's Footsteps _____

It is not until the moment when I have finished listening to the Psalms spoken by Christ, when I have heard each word resonate in his mouth, when I have managed to take hold of all the nuances and harmonies as he makes them sound, when my heart has become enflamed—not until then can I finally appropriate the Psalms for my own prayer, following him. Then, there can be no doubt, prayer will be what it has never been before; it will be aflame with fire. If it takes a whole lifetime to get there, how little that matters! What could possibly be more important? "If you wish to become a monk, said Abba Joseph of Panepho, become a fire! Then the old man stood up to pray and his fingers became like ten flaming lamps" (Apophthegms 389 and 390). This is the fire that Jesus came to light upon earth.

Right here is man's splendor, when prayer is a fire in God's presence, when the Book of Psalms is a fire in the heart. Such prayer is ignited by that of Christ. "While Jesus was praying," Luke tells us, "the aspect of his face was changed and his clothing became dazzling white"

(Luke 9:29). It is in Christ that prayer our splendor; it is in Christ too that the beauty of God takes substance.

On a number of occasions the evangelists say that Jesus prayed, but most often they say nothing more; the words of his prayers are rarely stated. Where are they? For the most part, in the Book of Psalms. Everything that is missing from Jesus's prayer in the New Testament is in Psalms. This book is the prayer book of Christ, a book, indeed, that is larger than any of the gospels.

If I know how to listen to Christ pray, then I can learn how to pray. I—who was afraid of my mistaken notions about God, I—can follow Christ with confidence because he knows God's heart, and he alone knows the way which leads there. He alone knows how to say the things I at times dare not say: "Lord, I love you!" or "My God, my God, why have you forsaken me?" Although these phrases at times feel awkward on my lips, in him I can learn their real significance. It is indeed to him above all that we must listen before we set ourselves to pray the psalms.

Let us be silent and contemplate the one in whom is revealed the splendor of both humanity and God.

In Christ the Difficulties of Prayer Are Lifted . . . _____

Slowly, the Book of Psalms becomes something completely different to us. The Father there provides the words for our prayers and the Son comes to pray them alongside us. The Father gives us the instructions of love and the Son comes alongside to practice them. The Father gives us David as a prayer companion, and David effaces himself before the Son, in whom he recognizes his Lord.

This is where we are in our engagement with the Book of Psalms, with Christ in view, in prayer; we listen to him and proceed with restraint. Jesus took Peter, James and John with him to pray, while in the Psalms it is us he takes along. He took Peter, James and John with him to pray in the uncreated light of the Transfiguration and also in the darkness of Gethsemane, the summit of light and the chasm of darkness. He does the same with us in the Psalms, where we too experience the summit and the chasm, the two extremes. Without him, the excess of light is too much, impenetrable, and the same with the depth of darkness. Without him, the excess of light turns us away as surely as the darkness. Without him, the Book of Psalms is a mountain range of impassable difficulties, and it is an all too common folly on our part to take it upon ourselves to enter it unaccompanied. We should therefore stay by his side to hear him pray and thus surmount the obstacles with him.

. . . in the Light of the Cross

Jesus's prayer is similar to his life: it is a pathway that leads to the heart of God; but, as we know, on this pathway we face, unavoidably, the cross, with the empty tomb beyond. As we listen to Christ pray, we cannot ignore the cross; listening to him pray, in fact, means above all taking a position before the cross with its face of darkness and its face of light . . . Then everything slowly becomes clear.

At la Trappe they have a most beautiful practice. On Good Friday, the whole community gathers in the church, in front of a cross and spends the greater part of the day reading the Psalms together. In front of the cross . . . ! A spiritual exercise like this has an amazing power, as though the Book of Psalms is finally in its rightful place. Everything that might appear excessive in the Psalms is no longer so before the cross; or rather, the Psalms fit right in with the cross, fit the excessive nature of the cross! For me this is how the difficulties of the Psalms little by little fade away, not just in a day, to be sure! I have not still reached the end of understanding the Psalms through the cross, but we will try, together, to read them in this way, at the foot of the cross . . .

The Psalms of Innocence _____

The first difficulty we will tackle is of the sort in which the light is too great. There are psalms which rather surprise, in which David loftily declaims his innocence:

> *The Lord has given me the reward of clean hands*
> *Because I have kept the ways of the Lord,*
> *And have never betrayed my God.*
> *His judgments are always before me,*
> *I have never turned away from his laws.*
> *I am blameless before him,*
> *I have kept myself far from sin.*
> *The Lord has rewarded me according to my righteousness,*
> *According to the purity of my hands, which I stretch out towards him.*
> (Ps 18:21–25)

How could I ever say words like this, I who know only too well what a sinner I am? If I appropriate this psalm to pray it, I could only stutter to a halt in midflow, not daring to go on with the prayer!

Indeed it would be best to stop here—not to close the book in discouragement but rather to listen to Christ pray this psalm. Then the words become clear; then they ring out with justice and truth in his mouth. I hear the innocence of the only one who is truly innocent before God. I listen to the only one who can pray in this way.

Then, following Christ to the cross, I discover that on the cross he justifies me by taking my sin. I discover that on the cross he makes me into a new creature, now innocent thanks to him. In Christ, I am innocent. In Christ, I too can speak to God in this same innocence, not by the innocence of my actions, my works, or my thoughts, but by the innocence I receive from Christ, given to me as a gift of pure grace and which I assume like the white garments of baptism.

Now, in Christ, I no longer hesitate to make the words of the psalm mine; in Christ I can pray them truthfully. If I don't do so, it is perhaps because I don't take seriously enough the innocence received from Christ. To pray these words is to honor the gift of Christ; it is to honor Christ, it is to take the cross seriously and contemplate Christ. We thus see how considering Christ on the cross enables us to enter into this aspect of the Book of Psalms and receive the excess of light, and how too the Book of Psalms teaches us to enter into the mystery of Christ to contemplate him, the innocent one who makes us innocent.

The Psalms of Repentance

In contrast, we have the psalms where sins are confessed, in which we fully recognize ourselves. With these, we easily throw ourselves into them, make them our own and pray them. Again, this precipitousness is not good and in fact presents a danger, that of shutting ourselves up within them, of becoming prisoners to our guilt and being crushed by it. These psalms speak of our sin, but they don't tell us what God's response is. How can we know if our sin is forgiven? The psalms take place in a silence which has the potential to overwhelm, a silence in which God's forgiveness is unheard and which gives free course to the morbidity of our guilt. This is why precipitous appropriation of them is not good.

To listen to these psalms as in the mouth of Christ does not immediately resolve the difficulty. How, indeed, could he, being without sin, confess faults that he has not committed?

But if we place ourselves before the cross, all becomes clear. On the cross, Christ bears our sin; on the cross he confesses our faults and frees us from them by his death. On the cross we receive from the Father the pardon asked of him by the Son, so it is here, at the foot of the cross, that we can confess the faults that he assumes; we can confess them with the certainty of pardon; we are forgiven with the forgiveness Christ receives from the Father.

Once more, it is before the cross that we can speak these psalms after hearing them on the lips of the Crucified One. Once again, the Book of Psalms enables us to enter the mystery of the cross, there to ponder the innocent sufferer who obtains our pardon.

"At once, both sinner and justified," as Luther forcefully states it. This indeed is the truth; we are both at once and can speak with equal truth the psalms of innocence and those of confession. They can only be spoken with the cross in view because it is at the cross that the tension between these two opposing dimensions of our being is resolved, the two realities of our existence: the old man and the new.

The Psalms of Suffering

Certain psalms describe the highest degree of suffering, depths of pain with physical details beyond anything we may have experienced:

> *I am poured out like water,*
> *All my bones are out of joint.*
> *My heart melts like wax within me*
> *And sinks into my bowels.*
> *My strength is dried up like clay,*
> *My tongue clings to the roof of my mouth . . .*
> *I can count all my bones.* (Ps 22:15–18)

To physical pain like this is added moral pain:

> *I am reproached by the people and despised,*
> *All who see me, mock me,*
> *They snigger and shake their heads.* (Ps 22:7–8)

Again,

43

Every night I cry aloud on my bed,

I water my couch with my tears,

My eyes are consumed with grief. (Ps 6:7–8)

So many other psalms expand on the theme, detailing sufferings of great diversity. On occasion we might recognize ourselves in some detail or other, but we cannot really take these psalms as our own; they are excessive.

Before the cross nothing is excessive or extreme; everything is to be measured against what we hear from the Crucified One. It is not the detail of what he went through as expressed in the words, but the abyss of suffering that he knows. Faced with the cross I am reduced to silence before the words that he alone can speak truthfully, without exaggeration or excess.

Compassion

After hearing such words on the lips of Christ, I certainly have no desire to make these sufferings my own, to appropriate these psalms. Instead the cross opens me up to another reality, namely, the suffering of some of those around me, certain of my brothers and sisters, men and women who do know what it is to count their own bones, whose tongues do cling to the roofs of their mouths, who cry aloud each night, who are rejected by their own . . . Through the cross I become attuned to these heights of suffering; they are illuminated for me by the suffering of the crucified Christ.

The suffering of such ones is at times so great that they can no longer speak of it, are unable to pray . . . But we can say these psalms for them, in the sight of the cross, which opens us to compassion; we pray them in Christ, who suffers in each suffering person, since each is a member of his suffering body. At the cross, the only truly compassionate one is the one crucified there, carrying in himself the suffering of all. With the cross in view, the psalms take our focus away from ourselves, emptying us of self and immersing us in Christ, in openness to others, in true compassion. At the cross, we learn that we are not the center of our own narrow prayers, but that the real center is Christ and his body. In the light of the cross, the Psalms bring us into the mystery of compassion and intercession.

Intercession

At first sight intercession seems to be only marginally present in the Psalms, and this may shock. "Save your people, bless your heritage, watch over them, carry them always" (Ps 28:9). Phrases like this are rather rare.

Where we are shocked by the limited place given to intercession, this is because we think of intercession as prayer that is only expressed in the third person: "I pray for him, for her, for them . . ." But there is another form of intercession, stated in the first-person plural, "we." It is precisely this form which is found to be most present in the Book of Psalms. The "we" of the Book of Psalms is most frequently a "we" of intercession.

Such is the case with Psalm 123, which is spoken by just one person ("I lift my eyes to you," v. 1) but extends to all those for whom the psalmist prays: "Have mercy upon us, O Lord, have mercy upon us; our soul is filled with contempt." This is a form of intercession which is founded on communion and sets forward this sense of solidarity and compassion. This is a type of intercession frequently to be found in the Bible and is taken up by Jesus when he teaches us to pray, "*Our* Father . . . give *us our* daily bread . . ." We may have no lack of bread, but we can pray all the same in fellowship with those who do, and this is intercession. When intercession is in the third person, this maintains a certain distance, and expresses compassion poorly. When intercession is in the first person, the distance is gone and gives full place to compassion. The Lord's Prayer is par excellence the prayer of compassion.

Christ's intercession is true compassion. On the cross he experienced this compassion in his flesh. In Christ, we may enter the same compassion, and without it our intercession risks being nothing more than the expression of our own sterile sensibilities. In Christ, our intercession is joined with his, and so reaches right to the heart of God.

Psalms of Violence against Enemies . . . ⸻

The major obstacle met with in the psalms today, one which has impelled many a Christian to renounce praying them, lies in the invectives against enemies. This is a substantial question, an unhappy question that we cannot and should not put to the side. We will try to advance in stages, suggesting signs to mark our route.

"But I say to you, love your enemies" (Matt 5:44). This word of Christ's must be our starting point and none other. It is a statement that must lie behind all our prayers, including the praying of the psalms. It is an inescapable precept: "Bless those who curse you; do good to those who hate you; pray for those who mistreat and persecute you."

. . . Enemies Both Human and Spiritual ⸻

We need to turn our attention to the word "enemy." The word covers all sorts of realities that the cross, again, enables us to distinguish, thereby alleviating the difficulties met with in the Psalter. It is in the light of the cross that we should proceed.

On the cross, then, Jesus prays for those who mistreat him and in this way he practices the love that he requires of us. "Father, forgive them, they know not what they do" (Luke 23:34). This is the prayer of Christ for those who despise, insult, injure, mistreat him . . . This is his

46

love for his enemies, those who crucified him, and for which we should be grateful since we too, in some form, were among them.

I too crucify Christ through my sinful actions, and I too am a beloved enemy of Christ; and I too am forgiven.

In short, the love of the enemy Jesus requires is practiced by him, right here in his passion; this is what engages us as we contemplate of the cross.

Nevertheless, this same cross leads us to uncover another reality that we should take time to examine if we are not to become confused as to the nature of our enemies. The cross shines a light that should be habitual to our thinking and that causes us to gain true spiritual discernment, discernment that gets to the core of things.

"On the cross, Christ killed enmity,"[1] Paul tells us in Ephesians 2:16. What is this saying? On one hand, Jesus prays for those who hate him, and on the other he slays hatred; all this on the same cross! Jesus does good to his enemies who hate him; and he kills another enemy, which is to say, hatred. The verb used is "kill," and unequivocally means "fight," "commit violence," "murder," without the slightest trace of love. How could love love hatred?

This is the distinction the cross provides us. For Christ there are two types of enemy: those of flesh and blood, which is to say, people; and enemies that are more subtle and abstract, not flesh and bone but no less real, such as hatred. This distinction, valuable for Christ, is not less so for us; we too, while we are to love our enemies, are not to love hatred! This is fundamental and most illuminating for our Christian life. "Love your enemies" concerns personal enemies, human persons, flesh and blood, the neighbor downstairs or the colleague at work . . . "Love your enemies" does not concern the abstract enemies, abstract entities which are no less real or powerful, such as hate. Who would say that a Christian must love hate?

With this background we can better understand Jesus's prayer on the cross. "Forgive them, they know not what they do." This "they know

1. French *haine*: enmity, hatred (Trans.).

47

not what they do" designates the people who crucified Christ. "They know not what they do" also implies that these men were animated by a stronger power, manipulated by another enemy who did know what he was doing, that is to say, the Enemy, with a capital letter, as Jesus designated Satan (Matt 13:39).

We thus need to distinguish between people, who don't know what they are doing in crucifying Christ, and the Enemy who manipulates them, just as he manipulated Judas. On one hand we have Judas, not knowing what he is doing until, too late, he opens his eyes and is unable to bear the remorse that seizes him; on the other, Satan, who knows just what he is doing. He had awaited the hour of the passion from the time of the temptation, as Luke specifies at the end of the temptation account: "Satan left him for a more favorable moment" (4:13). The long-awaited favorable moment was the passion; "Satan then entered Judas who went out to betray Jesus" (Luke 22:3). "Satan entered into Judas," well expresses the way Judas was unwittingly manipulated.

Satan, the Enemy, is the personal form of the abstract spiritual reality that we see in "hatred." The personification underlines the reality; we have to guard carefully against confounding Satan with people, the Enemy with our enemies.

As long as this distinction is clear and the cross is providing light by which we can discern between Satan and people, then we can return to the Psalms.

When Jesus sets forward Psalm 110 as we have seen in Matthew 2:42–44, the verse he cites is precisely a verse that mentions enemies: "The Lord said to my Lord, be seated at my right hand until I have made your *enemies* your footstool."

"*Your* enemies": this concerns Christ's enemies, but definitely not those for whom he asks pardon. "To have one's enemies as a footstool" is a very clear biblical expression that describes a crushing victory and definitely not an act of grace, compassion, forgiveness, or love. When he cites this verse, Jesus does not reject the military image; rather than correcting it, he keeps it. It is clear then that for him it has very real content and that the distinction remains between the enemies whom Jesus loves and whose feet he washes, and other enemies, enemies of a different type, whom he treads underfoot as a sign of victory.

The apostle Paul meditated at length the act of victory described in Psalm 110 precisely in order to identify the enemies concerned. He alludes to this verse in 1 Corinthians 15:25: "He must reign until all enemies are beneath his feet." The enemies in question Paul describes as "every dominion, authority and power" (15:24). Then he adds, "the last enemy to be destroyed is death" (15:26). There is no tenderness, compassion, pardon, or love for such enemies!

Those who will be beneath Christ's feet are not the Pharisees, the chief priests, Annas, Caiaphas, Judas, Pilate or the crowd of those who insulted and crucified him, but enemies of another order, spiritual powers. In Ephesians 1:22, the apostle returns to the same verse of Psalm 110, and gives the same explanation of it.

These enemy spiritual powers are designated in different ways in the New Testament. Luke calls them "the power of Satan" (Acts 26:18) or "the power of darkness" (Luke 22:53). In this he joins Paul, who writes, "God has delivered us from the power of darkness" (Col 1:13).

When Jesus saw Satan fall from heaven (Luke 10:18), he was not overcome with compassion to lift and console him! No; the following verse is of the essence because it concerns our own attitude with regard to the enemy: "Behold, said Jesus, I give you power to tread underfoot serpents and scorpions and all the power of the Enemy" (10:19). It is no longer Christ who treads underfoot the power of the Enemy but the disciples. We discover that the superiority of Jesus over the enemy is also given by him to his disciples; they are also to rule with authority and without compassion over all the power of the Enemy, and the Enemy in question is the one who fell from heaven, Satan. Christ causes his disciples to share in his victory, without asking that they love these scorpions, serpents, or other acolytes of Satan.

It is in just the same sense that we read from Paul's pen the following phrase, which implies a violence without the slightest compassion: "The God of peace will surely crush Satan under your feet!" (Rom 16:20). This is not just under Christ's feet but under ours too. We are not victorious in ourselves, but we are beneficiaries of the victory wrought by God alone. This verse from the Letter to the Romans is not one brought forward by those who complain about the violence in the Psalms, and yet it is speaking of the same violence—God's! The "God of peace"!

Strong in this assured future victory for Christians, Paul invites us to take up arms and go to war against the enemies of Christ, who are ours too (Eph 6:10–13): but there is no longer any question here, not the least doubt—these enemies are spiritual enemies and the combat in question is a spiritual combat. "We fight not against flesh and blood but against principalities, powers and rulers of the darkness here below, and against spirits of wickedness in heavenly places" (6:12).

I have taken my time over this, but I believe it to have been necessary; we need to guard against any confusion. The whole of the New Testament is clear (see again 1 Pet 3:22); it is unanimous in designating two types of enemy whom we must not confuse, under pain of severe consequences to the spiritual life. On one side we have personal enemies, those who are "flesh and blood," as Paul says in Ephesians 6:12; these enemies must above all be loved, and that unconditionally. On the other side are the spiritual enemies, those invisible to us and who are to be fought absolutely. This is where the true spiritual combat lies.

The Spiritual Combat

Before returning to the psalms and the conflicts they describe, there are a few more words that it seems important to say, as they will bring still more clarity to this issue of our enemies.

These spiritual enemies that are so hard to pin down—where exactly are they? They are all around, both in people and outside them, but above all we should say, in us. We are talking first about the passions, the "evil thoughts" of which we have already spoken, adverse thoughts, but also those impulses, reactions, which turn us against God and incite us not to love, either God or our neighbor.

The church Fathers, following Paul, insist on the fact that spiritual combat must first be conducted within ourselves before we begin to meddle with the evil thoughts of our neighbor. This is the issue of the speck and the beam in the eye, and it is foundational.

Paul speaks of this battle within himself and in this respect discusses "the sin that lives in me" (Rom 7:17 and 20). A few verses further on, the apostle says to the Romans, "the Spirit of God lives in you" (8:9 and 11). The contrast is very eloquent; in me, says Paul, dwells evil, but in you Romans dwells the Holy Spirit! The inward look invites struggle; looking at the other person is a look of love and peace. Paul is well aware that the Holy Spirit lives in him too, just as he does in the Romans, and that evil is to be found in them too, but he localizes the place of combat as being in himself; he therefore so expresses himself as to convey that each person must engage in spiritual combat in their own life, not in those of others.

Spiritual combat is always a personal battle to the point that some people, the better to conduct it, have withdrawn to the desert, as Jesus did to combat Satan. A solitary battle it certainly is, but happily, with Jesus's help! In the solitude of the desert, discernment becomes clearer.

With regard to this discernment, here are a few points to note, a few errors to avoid.

- "Sin dwells in me," but I am not sin. Sin dwells in me, but I need not identify myself with it. We can say that evil is my tenant, and that is all—a tenant that is obstructive and violent, undesirable and hateful, but a tenant. Sin is in me and I am a sinner, but a sinner whom God loves, not sin, which God rejects. I am a sinner, but not sin; if this distinction is not made, the whole spiritual life becomes chaos.

– "Sin dwells in me." We cannot consider ourselves as safe from it, unconcerned about it, innocent of everything it leads us to do, beyond reproach; this would be a very naïve spiritual blindness. I am a sinner, whose every repentance is welcomed by God with mercy.

– While sin is in me, it is not to be confused with the body, in an opposition of body and soul; this would be to make the invisible enemy visible and palpable. The early Fathers in their asceticism did poorly in adopting a negative attitude to the body. We need not, however, fall into the same error, but can follow the later Fathers, who did not make this confusion. When Paul says "I treat my body rigorously"[2] (1 Cor 9:27), he is not treating his body as an enemy so much as an ally that will help in his spiritual combat rather than betray him through laziness or complicity with this or that enemy passion The passage where Paul expresses himself in this way is clearly focused on sporting images in which the apostle compares himself with an athlete. There is no one more ascetic than a sportsman; he also "treats his body rigorously," with the goal of victory, a victory which is won precisely by the body and not against it. In the spiritual fight, it is the whole being which is engaged, the soul and the body, together.

In Christ, the Enemies in the Psalms Are Spiritual _____

Fortified by this distinction between the enemies to be loved and those to be combated, we can now return to the Book of Psalms. The psalms never speak of love for one's enemies; they always locate us in

2. A still more literal translation of the author's French might say "harshly"; both are nearer the Greek than the usual English rendering of "subduing" or "disciplining" the body; the Greek seems to have the idea of "buffet." A lengthy, very fine account of "Asceticism" is to be found in the author's book of that title, translated as *Spiritual Discipline, a Way of Liberty* (Trans.).

relation to them as in a situation of conflict, without love, compassion, or forgiveness. From this fact, all the Fathers, in line with the New Testament, reasoned that we should usually think of Psalms as speaking of spiritual enemies rather than personal enemies ("of flesh and blood"), even if this is not always clear in some particular psalm. What is not clear in Psalms becomes clear from the perspective of the New Testament, in the light of the cross. Once again, it is only before the cross that we can understand the psalms and pray them. Without this light it is no longer possible to pray the psalms. Reader friend, feel free to forget everything I say, but not this: without the light of the cross, praying the psalms is impossible!

To pray the psalms with the idea that they mainly concern spiritual enemies is not forcing the text. In fact some of the psalms are very clear about this. For example, in Psalm 55, the enemies described are not people but sinful passions:

> *I see discord and violence in the city.*
>
> *Day and night they go about upon the ramparts;*
>
> *Within, crime and wickedness; ruination is everywhere;*
>
> *Fraud and brutality never leave its streets.* (55:10–12)

This passage describes people walking about on the ramparts of the city and others in the streets, but they are personifications of "discord," "violence," "fraud," "brutality," of spiritual enemies to be fought, and in no way are they enemies of flesh and blood.

Elsewhere in the psalms, the enemies are often described as savage animals, which is another descriptive image of spiritual enemies, as is seen again in the New Testament where we find "scorpions and serpents"; indeed, the Old Testament had prepared us for this from the outset of Genesis. The first appearance of the Enemy in Genesis is in the guise of a serpent, and it is a question with him of "enmity" (Gen 3:15). This talking snake is surely something other than a new species for the zoologists, to be placed in the correct class of serpent! A little further, in the story of Cain and Abel, sin is described as an animal, lying at the door of Cain's heart (4:7). This "personification" of spiritual enemies as animals returns frequently in the psalms. Thus, in Psalm 22, we have the impression of being in the midst of a veritable jungle in which there appear dogs, lions, buffaloes and bulls (vv. 12, 13, 20, 21); it is clear though that these are not literal. Who has ever seen wild cats and bulls become allies and working together? This detail shows that the psalmist is concerned with other adverse realities. In Psalm 35, these same enemies are described both as lions which tear (vv. 15, 17) and as men who mock (v. 16).

In brief, the Book of Psalms calls us in a number of ways not to read too quickly, not to be limited to a simplistic approach and so mistake the true nature of our enemies. If there are other verses that lead to confusion and potentially leave us believing human enemies are in view, we must not attribute this to the psalms, but to our approach. It is not the Book of Psalms which is obscure but our understanding; the problem lies not in the Psalms but in our lack of spiritual discernment, a discernment which needs to be trained by the New Testament. If we have difficulty praying the psalms, we need to silently return to the foot of the cross and listen to them in the mouth of the one who put hatred to death and who crushed underfoot serpents, scorpions and all the power of Satan. We must allow Christ to transform our outlook and give us discernment between those enemies who are to be loved and those who are to be fought. Then we can take up the psalms once more and pray them, aware that the only adversaries in them to be cursed are the spiritual enemies.

> *O Babylon the wretched!*
>
> *Happy is he who repays you the evil done us;*
>
> *Happy is he who takes your infants and dashes them against the rock!*

Babylon here (Ps 137:8, 9) could only be the Enemy, Satan! If not, I must absolutely zip my mouth! The enemies are the multitude of adverse thoughts that rise up in us and alienate us from God. To pray this verse to curse some enemy of flesh and blood is a spiritual nonsense, a grave mistake.

Another example to lead us further away from misunderstanding: thanks to Romans 16:20 ("The God of peace will shortly crush Satan under your feet") we can understand the following verse—"God shall break the head of the one (Satan) who hates him" (Ps 68:21). If we read this text in a different way, and see God breaking the head of men, we need to stop and return to the cross.

In Christ, We Can Pray the Psalms of Violence _____

Along with the Fathers I am making the case for praying all these psalms, but with the absolute condition of being conscious of the reality of the spiritual struggle, and engaging in it without confusing human and spiritual enemies; otherwise we should not pray them.

For anyone who has integrated this reality of spiritual combat into their spiritual life, praying these psalms brings with it great benefit; it allows us, in fact, to speak to God, without inhibition, of the daily warfare we experience, with the violence that implies. The psalms provide the words we at times have difficulty finding, and thanks to them we can put words to all the adverse thoughts that assail us. Further, the psalms help us to be thoroughly aware that the spiritual Enemy is not some weakling we can simply shrug off, but that his ruses outstrip our imagination in deviousness; he can turn up on the doorstep as an ally so close that we share our bread with him. The Book of Psalms also demonstrates that it is most often preferable to flee this adversary as too tricky, and to take refuge close to God, whose support and help are unfailing, a great rock, a fortress. The Psalms as a whole teach us that though we may at times suffer a defeat, it is never total, and never to the point of despair; that Christ has victoriously undergone the same struggles, and causes us to share in his victory. In this way, individual psalms become luminous. They don't, in their violence, shake our faith in God's love; on the contrary, they strengthen it. This all takes place as we ponder the cross which enables us to discern the real enemies to be fought.

There are religious communities that have decided to parenthesize in their Psalters all the violent passages and not read them during the course of their offices. This decision seems sensible to me in so far as those attending their services may not be prepared for prayer of the psalms. It is kind and fraternal not to scandalize those who are unprepared; but this does not mean that in the same communities these psalms of violence might not very well be prayed outside the offices, during times of personal prayer, in the light of the cross, along the lines proposed in the New Testament and by the Fathers.

When Supplication Turns into Praise

There is another difficulty with the psalms, less brutalizing and imposing than those to do with enemy powers, more hidden but no less present; a difficulty which all the same can stop us in our tracks and be something of an enigma that holds us back from truly entering into praying the psalms. This difficulty has to do with what I call the turning point of a psalm; let me explain.

Certain psalms begin with a lengthy and intense supplication, at times accompanied by imprecations against enemies, and then suddenly, without the least explanation, break into uninterrupted praise until the close of the psalm.

Psalm 28 is a good example. Supplication takes up the first three verses; the following two verses turn to imprecation; and then verse 6 shakes us with the newness of its tone: "Blessed be the Lord who has heard the voice of my prayer!" What happened? How had God intervened? What had he done to produce this sudden outburst of praise? What did he do, for David to so suddenly start praising him before he even finishes his prayer of request? It's not as though we are thinking about two psalms, one following hard after the other and God's intervention, but of one psalm on its own, prayed in a single breath! I would love to know, to be able to pray this psalm and likewise pass from supplication to praise.

In the second verse, David pleads: "Listen to the voice of my supplication." In verse 6, he blesses: "He has heard the voice of my supplication." The words are the same, underlining their perfect fulfilment by God, but the psalm says nothing about what took place; David does not explain how he knows that his prayer is answered. How does he know? This is an important question for our spiritual life, since it concerns the fulfilment of prayer.

Not only had God listened but he had intervened in a concrete way. In fact, at the beginning of the psalm, David speaks of the tomb, leaving the impression he is danger of dying: "If you keep silence I will go down into the tomb." Then, in verse 7, he gives thanks for God's help: "He has helped me." God, then, had delivered David from a danger unknown to us but real. The issue is not to know more about this danger but more about God's intervention, an intervention so sudden that David can only forgo his supplication for praise, and his imprecation in favor of intercession: "Save your people, bless your inheritance, watch over them and bear them up forever" (v. 9). Ending as it does like this, the psalm leaves us a little disconcerted!

The same difficulty appears in other psalms. Thus Psalm 13, which is entirely a lament except for the final verse, which, without explanation, says, "I will sing to the Lord for all the good he has done to me." What is this "good he has done to me"? What had God done? This psalm, like others, passes from its closing praise into silence without having given any indication or explanation of God's saving intervention that excited the praise.

God's intervention at times is such as to leave the impression that it precedes the end of the supplication. David says this:

> *When I lifted my cry towards him*
>
> *My mouth was already shouting his praise.* (Ps 66:17)

Word for word this says:

As my mouth cried out to him

Praise arose on my tongue.

This is to say that praise was rising up within me, even as I was still pleading! For exegetes of the psalms, these are enigmas . . .

If we look for a precise event in the life of the psalmist, it will never be found! I believe that where David declines to tell what God had done, it is because he can't explain it. We doubtless have to look for God's intervention at another level, more personal; certainly God intervenes in the most timely way in the externalities of life, through events that we can recount, but he also steps in at a more profound level, so profound that it is practically impossible to tell. What I am saying here, reader friend, requires a discernment that I lack, so for this reason I am asking your indulgence. What can we say about God's intervention in the depths of our spiritual life? I sense it; I glimpse it confusedly; I can see just enough of it to point it out; may the Lord illumine you to see it more clearly than me.

We might think that David experienced a "visitation" from God, one of those indescribable spiritual experiences that draw forth overflowing praise; but if this were so, we would no doubt find two psalms, one before and another after the experience, not just the one.

The difficulty that these turning points in a psalm represent with their transformation into praise once again invites us to be silent and contemplate the cross, to turn towards Christ to hear such psalms as he would speak them. Then everything will become clear, as was the case with other difficulties.

The Cross: From Supplication to Praise _____

We know that on the cross Christ prayed Psalm 22. The evangelists give us only the first verse of the psalm, but it is clear that he prayed the whole of it, though he may not have given expression to it all out loud: "My God, my God, why have you forsaken me?" And then he must have continued . . .

The fact of Jesus praying this psalm on the cross is very precious to us at this point because it is another psalm that suddenly changes direction. Up to verse 22 it is all supplication; then suddenly it changes, and not in the space between two verses on this occasion (as in 28:6–7), not in between the two halves of a verse (as in 13:6), but in midphrase! Here is the verse in its entirety:

> *Save me from the mouth of the lion*
> *From the horns of the ox . . .*
> *You have answered me.* (22:21)

The reversal could not be more sudden! All the following verses are praise that flows into silence without the slightest explanation or indication of the contents of God's response . . . ! We see that on the cross Jesus experienced the change which concerns us, the turning point from supplication to praise.

The change is so abrupt that many translators have not thought it appropriate to translate what is nonetheless perfectly clear in the Hebrew. Such translators have generally at this point followed the most ancient of the translations, the Greek of the Septuagint: "Save me from the mouth of the lion and from the horns of the unicorn regard my lowliness."[3] The change of direction is less violent but is still present because the ensuing verses are nothing but praise.

We however will stay with the Hebrew: "You have answered me."

"You have answered me," not "you're about to answer me" or "you will answer me"; no, it is, "you have answered me," right at the point I am dying, forsaken by you!

The psalm says nothing more about God's response, nothing of his intervention, and I believe there is nothing that could be said because there are no words to explain the inexplicable. God's intervention is

---

3. Thus the Brenton English translation of the Septuagint (Trans.).

beyond our understanding. The absence of words to express it does not mean it is not present, just beyond our grasp.

We will not find the explanation in the psalm but in the fact that it was spoken by Christ on the cross, and it is as we ponder the cross that we can understand the psalm. God's answer—is the cross; God's intervention is the cross and nothing else, and it is beyond our understanding.

The cross is a historical event that can be recounted for sure, but much more; it is an event whose real profundity escapes us. The cross itself is a tipping point; it is at once the source of the infinite suffering of being abandoned, as well as God's answer to every prayer. It is the extreme depth of supplicating cry, as well as the subject for the praise of the entire cosmos. It is the turning point of Christ's life, as it is for every spiritual life, at a level no word will ever be able to say with exactitude.

What took place during God's intervention at the heart of Psalm 22? What happened was the cross . . .

The Darkness of Hell

When Christ cried from the cross, "My God, my God, why have you forsaken me?" he was speaking from the heart of darkness (Matt 27:45–46), out of the darkness which three hours earlier had invaded the earth. The psalm sounds out from the darkness and the darkness imparts added intensity to the complaint. The darkness wrenches the cry from Jesus.

The darkness is the sign that hell had invaded earth. The earth was subjected at midday to the power of darkness, which imposed itself without opposition. Jesus had announced this the evening before on the Mount of Olives: "Now is your hour, the power of darkness" (Luke 22:53). This darkness is the darkness of hell, as is readily understood from Job 10:21–22, Ps 88:10–12, Matt 8:12 . . . Only in hell are lions and oxen united against their victim. Jesus has already descended into the maw of hell and it is from the depths of that darkness, when the whole earth becomes a hell, that he "cried out with a loud voice, My God, my God, why have you forsaken me?" The whole of this hell-entangled earth resonated with his cry! There could be no deeper cry of supplication; an abyss . . .

It is precisely here, at this, the very heart of darkness, that we find the turning point; it is at the heart of the darkness that God intervenes against the power of Satan, against the power of darkness. But our eyes are not such as to be able to see, not at the center of such darkness; neither can we describe what took place.

Luminous Darkness

The darkness is also the dwelling place of God. In the darkness he approaches, surrounded by it, and draws near to the cross. In the darkness is God's hidden presence, a presence beyond grasp or description, but a presence which saves.

To properly understand the link between the darkness and the presence of God we can remind ourselves of what was said by men of God like Solomon ("The Lord chooses to dwell in the darkness"; 1 Kgs 8:12) and David ("He makes the darkness his secret place"; Ps 18:11; "Darkness and clouds surround him"; Ps 97:2); "Moses drew near to the thick darkness where God was" (Exod 20:21). Clearly, God finds it good to dwell in the darkness.

This does not prevent us from saying that God is light, but his light is so intense that for us it is darkness!

This is the reality of the darkness of the cross, a double reality. This darkness is both the arrogance of the power of Satan and the lowly, discreet but saving presence of God. Christ, at the heart of the darkness can say both, "Why have you forsaken me?" and "You have heard me!"

Only Christ could perceive the thickness of the darkness, the depth of hell and the tangible presence of God. He alone experiences at once both abandonment and presence, the abandonment by and the response of the Father. The darkness pulls out of him from the cross his cry of "Why"; and the same darkness, at the same time, gives him the answer. At the same time! There couldn't be a more precise point of balance . . .

As my mouth cried out to him
Praise arose on my tongue.

This turning point that we are trying to take hold of is really beyond reach since its place is in the darkness, and also beyond reach because of its twofold nature and great depth. The cross indeed speaks both of the depth of hell and the depth of God's heart.

It is beyond our grasp because it is the point where eternity enters history and also where history enters the eternal. It is forever beyond reach for us as long as we remain bound by history, but still it is the point on which the psalm turns, something of which we can have only an imprecise intuition.

What more can be said?

This moment where everything changes is the point at which a sinner steps into justification—me too! It is the moment Jesus experienced on the cross and which we experience in the light of the cross. It is the moment of life which cannot be described; not, in a sense, a historical event in life but one which is inscribed into it, underlying personal history, at a level so deep that it has transformed life and illuminates it. It is a moment which escapes our grasp but makes things clear; a moment which is inaccessible to the conscious mind but one to which our heart attests and which it celebrates; one that God alone knows in its truth since he is its author, but which nonetheless causes us to sing. It is indeed a moment that brings us up short in our supplication and causes us to say, "You have answered me," and fills us with praise to the point of silent worship. It is a moment in life that escapes any description such as could be written into one's memoirs, a moment that already belongs to eternity. A moment that cannot be grasped but which has taken hold of us forever . . .

What more to say?

It is the point at which the thief enters paradise, though still on the cross. Is not this astonishing? In response to the plea of this condemned man, Jesus draws him that very day into paradise (Luke 23:42–43). This "today" of his response is the eternal today of God in the thief's own history. For him too his life is transformed, just as is the psalm on the cross; he cries out and immediately is able to praise God as he sees the gates of paradise open:

> I said, the darkness will crush me,
>
> But even the night is become light around me.
>
> The darkness with you is not dark
>
> And the night is light as the day! (Ps 139:11–12)

It is the point at which the death of Christ has already become the power of the resurrection. How else can we explain how, right at the moment of Christ's death, the graves were opened, "and many bodies of the saints that were dead revived" (Matt 27:52)? It is the point at which death and resurrection are no longer separate with this breaking in of eternity. Christ himself died from before all eternity, and was raised for all eternity.

With the Crucified One's cry, Satan reaches the peak of his power; it is the pinnacle of the power of darkness. But the weakness of Christ is so great that the darkness falls open, the veil of the Temple is split and the earth trembles. It is the weakness of the Almighty, the weakness of Christ, who snatches the dead from the power of Satan! It is the moment at which the weakness of Christ is Almighty, the power of life over the power of hell, which cannot resist. The foolishness of God, wiser than the wisdom of men and women! The profound depths of foolish wisdom . . .

It is the moment when the darkness shines with the greatest light, uncreated light, uncreated light which for us is darkness. At the heart of the darkness, the light of the world is hung on a cross; there is darkness at midday, the sun eclipsed by eternal light. Never was there light so great as in that darkness, because it is the light of God, crucified light open to view, silent light which takes the world into its crucible and wraps around it like a cloak.

"Luminous darkness" the Fathers say! Some of them took this as their starting place to ponder the cross. Happy are those whose eyes are open. Happy are those whose ears are open to the depth of the cry from the cross ("My God, my God, why have you forsaken me?") but also to the sound of God's silence . . . "You have answered me . . . !"

Christ alone could truthfully pray Psalm 22 and say in the same breath both "Why have you forsaken me?" and "You have answered me." No one other than Christ could pray this more than superficially. He alone can speak these psalms that turn from supplication to praise and from praise to silence. But in our turn, in his footsteps, in the luminous darkness of the cross, we can pray these psalms, enter into their lament and into their praise, allow ourselves to be gripped by their pleadings, and in Christ become people of praise.

This is the amazing depth of the Book of Psalms, this wonderful crucible in which the beauty of our being is fashioned, this astonishing school of prayer, whose doors open one by one onto the cross, where the Son, in prayer, leads us by his Spirit into the heart of God.

— CHAPTER 4 —

The Spirit Teaches Us to Pray

THROUGH CHRIST, OTHER ASPECTS of the Book of Psalms become clear in surprising ways; but, as these become clear, difficulties that were previously hidden and unsuspected, but nonetheless important for our spiritual lives, also begin to appear.

Satan Uses the Psalms

To our surprise then, we find that Satan himself thinks about the psalms, that he has engaged in reading them, not for purposes of prayer but in order to find ways to ensnare. This becomes evident in the account of Christ's temptation, in the face to face encounter between the two. When Satan invited Jesus to jump from the top of the Temple, he added: "because it is written, he will give his angels charge concerning you and they will bear you up with their hands lest you dash your foot against a rock" (Matt 4:6). He was citing a passage from Psalm 91 (vv. 11–12). If Satan was able to speak like this, it is because he had read the Book of Psalms; he had meditated in it, after his own way no doubt, but he had meditated it. I believe that he must know it by heart!

How troubling this is! What does it have to say to our reading of the Psalter? We receive the Psalms as a gift from God; they enable us to discover Christ's prayer, pure prayer, and now, to find that the same Book of Psalms is in Satan's mouth is an injection of trouble. Trouble is

65

just what Satan wants; in contrast, Christ desires not trouble but light, the light of his heartwarming teaching.

The account of the temptation is not intended to disturb us but to illuminate, to put us on our guard and invite us to draw nearer still to Christ.

Two Ways to Appropriate the Psalms

There are two ways to appropriate the psalms, Christ's way and the Enemy's. Our own way of using them will approximate one or the other according to the disposition of our heart. If we take hold of the Book of Psalms too quickly, we can naively do so erroneously and perversely; Christ alone can teach us to appropriate the psalms correctly and avoid the traps of the Adversary. It is important that we be alert to this, and understand why it is not good to use the Book of Psalms without having listened to Christ very closely. As we listen, we are encouraged to vigilance in the spiritual combat; this is not vigilance against "satanic verses" that the enemy might have sown into Psalms (tares among the good seed) but vigilance with regard to a particular way of appropriating and meditating.

We could easily use the Book of Psalms to reinforce our vices, and this is a perverse manner of making it our own. We could thus feed our own laziness with a verse like "God gives his beloved sleep" (Ps 127:2)! In Christ the light is focused not on our desire for sleep but on God's marvelous kindness. Man is encouraged to trust in rather than take advantage of God.

We could also, when tempted to sin, wind up accepting the tempter's suggestion, consoling ourselves in advance with the idea that God will necessarily pardon us, it being written that, "The Lord is slow to anger and full of love. . . He does not deal with us according to our offences" (Ps 103:8–10); this is another perverse usage which intends to submit God to our service.

Again, after some sin, I might despair of the divine pardon and capitulate in the struggle, given that it is written, "Behold, the evil doers are fallen; beaten down, they shall never rise" (Ps 36:12). Another perverse usage, which denies the depth of God's forgiveness.

These are different ways to fall into the Adversary's traps. In general, Christ places God at the center and serves him, encouraging us to do the same, whereas Satan suggests we put ourselves at the center and give free course to everything that agitates our impure hearts, even if this means using God and his word for our own ends.

Faced with the Adversary's nets, Anthony asked "Who can overcome this?" He heard a voice reply, saying, "Humility" (Apophthegm 7). That is the answer, and the voice is God's! In humility we must learn never to think of ourselves as strong enough to fight off the Adversary, or sufficiently clear-sighted to see through all his ruses; in humility, we unfailingly ask God for his help, even in the first impulse of prayer, worship: "O God, have mercy on me a sinner," said the publican (Luke 18:13). Every monastic office begins with a similar plea, which is both wisdom and humility: "O God, come to my aid, O Lord, come quickly to my help" (Ps 70:1).

We must never attempt to manage on our own and do without God's help, even if we feel strong, incisive, mature, spiritual . . . because Satan is trickier than we are; his preliminary ruse is to whisper into our ear that we are strong, insightful and spiritual! He is able to disguise himself as an angel of light and cloak his voice in a psalm of light.

The further we advance in the spiritual life, the more we need to turn to Christ to learn everything from him, including how to pray the psalms.

The account of the temptation shows us that while we have trouble discerning the tempter's tricks, Christ knows them all and thwarts them all. We can find refuge with Christ, as with a master. Would we be capable without Christ of discerning the voice of Satan behind that beautiful promise of God: "I will give the angels charge over you, to keep you in all your ways; they will bear you up in their hands lest you dash your foot against the rocks"?

Behind the sweet words, Christ was able to detect the voice of Satan. This is what he did with his disciple Peter, similarly detecting the voice of Satan behind the words, however well-intentioned they might have been. After Jesus's announcement of his passion, Peter generously stated his conviction that God would not leave the Christ to die in this way: "God forbid! This will never happen to you" (Matt 16:23). Lovely sentiments which might lead to magnificently compassionate prayer, but behind this reaction redolent of the best feelings Jesus discerns the voice of Satan. How many of our prayers, springing from the finest of our feelings, are booby-trapped by Satan, and mask his voice? We, in our spiritual blindness, can hardly begin to say. Prayer in Christ is what we need to learn. We realize that Satan can pervert our most beautiful prayers; prayer however should not seek to be beautiful, but to be in Christ; that is when it becomes beautiful, beautiful with his imprint upon it, not with our sentiments.

Prayer in Christ; this, I believe, means "prayer in the name of Jesus" (John 14:13–14). The expression is not the addition of a formula at the close of our prayers to lend it an air of conformity! It means praying with Christ's authority, in the light of his presence. In this way we can learn to pass every word in our prayers through the crucible of the word of Christ. It means speaking not, as Peter did, out of pure emotion or philanthropy, out of our brotherly concern, but bringing everything before the cross into the light of the resurrection; into the fire of refinement and humility, without which, in the guise of good thoughts, our prayer wanders into the snares of the Enemy.

As we do this, little by little, the enemies of which the psalms speak appear in the plain light of day; in this light we learn to recognize Satan and his henchmen. The Book of Psalms then supplies the words that enable us to give free rein to our violence against these foul intruders which go about to trap us in our spiritual lives.

Those that seek after my soul,

May they go down into the bowels of the earth,

May they be pierced through by the sword.

May they become the portion of wolves! (Ps 63:9–10)

It is against Satan and him alone that the maledictions of Psalms eventually gain their true meaning.

Not to take a step on the way of prayer alone—this is the intent of what I am saying. Again, it is just what we learn from the account of the temptation, where we find that Jesus himself did not go to meet the tempter alone. Indeed, when he pushes deep into the solitude of the desert to be tempted, the evangelists are unanimous in telling us that he was led there by the Holy Spirit (Matt 4:1; Mark 1:12; Luke 4:1). Where Christ discerns the presence of Satan, it is because the Spirit is with him, alongside him, in him. Discernment is a gift of the Spirit, a perfect gift for the person who does nothing without him. Christ and the Spirit are not separable; Christ's perfect discernment demonstrates this.

If Christ never stepped out alone, who are we to risk ourselves alone in our endeavors at spiritual life? To unceasingly invoke God's help means invoking the presence of Christ and the presence of the one who is always with him.

We have now reached a point of readiness for the final element of our approach to the psalms.

The Spirit Is Come to Teach Us to Pray

Who is it that is really speaking in the psalms? The question poses itself anew, as a fresh look at Psalms brings it back to the fore.

At a first reading, we saw that it is David who speaks in the Psalter. Then we noticed that through David it is Christ himself who is really speaking. Nevertheless, it is not so simple!

Clearly it is Christ who speaks Psalm 22: "My God, my God, why have you forsaken me?" He is also speaking in a number of other psalms which are stated in the first person, and we have just been considering at length Psalms in general as spoken by Christ; nevertheless, not all the psalms can be heard this way.

We find, in fact, psalms which are not spoken by Christ but are actually addressed to him, designating him by the second person ("you"); thus, Psalm 45:

> You are more beautiful than any of the sons of man,
> Grace is poured out on your lips:
> Therefore, God has blessed you forever . . .
> God, your God, has anointed you with the oil of gladness
> Above all your fellows. (45:3, 7)

These words are surely addressed to Christ and not to God, who is mentioned here as the one who has blessed and anointed Christ. This psalm, like others, is not from the lips of Christ but is spoken to him.

This is not all. Alongside the psalms where Christ speaks in the first person ("I"), and the psalms where he is designated by the second person ("You"), there are also psalms which concern Christ as the third person ("He"). This is seen in Psalm 110: "The Lord (= the Father) said to my Lord (= the Son)." It is the same in Psalm 72 or again in Psalm 84:

> God, you are our shield;
> Look upon the face of your Messiah. (84:10)

In short, Christ is "I" and "You" as well as "He" in the Book of Psalms.

As we continue reading the Book of Psalms we find that the first person is not always Christ. On occasion it is God the Father, as we have seen in Psalm 50:

Listen, my people, I am speaking;

Israel, you are my witness.

I, God, I am your God . . . (Ps 50:7)

However, as again we have seen, at times the Father is addressed in the second person:

Who is the Son of man that you *should care for him?*

You *have made him a little lower than God,*

You *have crowned him with glory and honor;*

You *have set him over all the works of* your *hands.* (Ps 8:5–7)

Who except the Father could be spoken of this way in connection with the Son? So the Father is designated by the second person, as is the case in many other psalms.

But the Father is also spoken of in the third person in still other psalms. This is the case in Ps 2:2, where this is just how it is designated, as is the Son:

The kings of the earth have set themselves,

The rulers have entered into a league

Against the Lord and his Messiah.

The same in 110:1

An oracle of the Lord, to my Lord.

In short, like the Son, we see that the Father is designated as "I" and "You" as well as "He," and this complicates the reading of the psalms not a little.

To top matters, despite all this, the Psalter remains the book of David's prayers in which he expresses himself in the first person, though effacing himself; and through him any person, including you and I, can pray. It is therefore I or you expressing self in the first person, as in Psalm 51 for example: "Have mercy on me, my God, according to your loving-kindness . . ."

In other psalms God addresses us, not Christ, in the second person:

Who are you to recite my laws

And have my covenant in your mouth,

You who love not correction

And cast my words far away from you? (Ps 50:16–17)

Lastly, God also speaks to people, addressing them in the third person: "Gather together before me my faithful ones" (Ps 50:5). It is clearly we who are in question with this mention of the "faithful ones."

In short, we see that we ourselves are designated in Psalms in the first person and the second as well as the third. To this we can add the fact that man expresses himself in the singular ("have mercy on me, my God" 51:3) and in the plural ("have mercy on us, O Lord, have mercy on us" 113:3).

By way of summarizing this excursion, we can say simply that it is not always easy to understand who is speaking in the psalms, God the Father, the Son, one man or many . . . ?

We can leave aside the fact that this difficulty is of great antiquity, and that as early as the Septuagint, before our era, there were often divergences from the Hebrew text in this area, verses being attributed to different speakers. Thus, in the Hebrew, verse 6 of Psalm 2 is spoken by the Father: "I have anointed my king on Zion, my holy mountain." In the Greek, by contrast, the same verse is seen as spoken by the Son: "I have been established by him as king on Zion, his holy mountain"!

We have to face up to this extreme diversity of speakers in Psalms. Who is really speaking through this prodigious variety? Perhaps this is a false question! In any case one alternative might be the following: perhaps the apparent parceling up of Psalms among different speakers is the final truth of it, to which we need to accommodate ourselves. Again, though, this may not be the case; perhaps there is the flashing of one singular, more profound light.

David Effaces Himself before the Holy Spirit . . . _____

The difficulty is resolved thanks to David himself, who gives us an answer speaking directly to this subject, not in the Book of Psalms but at the close of the second book of Samuel, in what are presented as his "last words" (23:1).

If we look closely, we find that in fact David has something more to say after these "last words," so that we need, no doubt, to understand by this expression, rather than his dying words, his spiritual testament, a summary of his life from the standpoint of a final analysis. Whatever the case may be, these "last words" are to be listened to with extreme attention. He says:

> *The Spirit of the Lord spoke in me*
> *His word on my tongue.* (23:2)

We have here an amazing confession such as few are able to make. In the mouth of some people this would be an expression of immense pride, but no doubt it cannot be understood in such a way coming from a man at whom we marvel for his self-effacement and humility. The last words of David, in the evening of his life, are rather to be understood as follows: "I am not the one who matters; don't think about me; pay no attention to me; rather, ponder the one who is greater than me and who has seen fit to put his holy word in my mouth, I who am so unworthy. This other one, who expresses himself and speaks through me, is the Holy Spirit."

This is David's summary of his life, made perhaps after many years of progressively greater discernment. This final confession was from that moment so clear to him as to perhaps be the reason he declined to put his name to a good number of psalms, thereby tacitly attributing them to their true author, the Holy Spirit.

. . . as Attested by the Ancients . . .

"The Spirit of the Lord spoke in me": whether this statement was humble or pretentious, there is that about it which might seem close to being a little crazy, so it needs to have been approved, accepted, attested and recognized by others if it is to be received as authentic.

This indeed is what happened. Long after his death, a few centuries later, perhaps at the time of the Temple reconstruction after the return from Babylon (though we don't really know exactly when or by whom), it was concluded that David had spoken truly and that the Holy Spirit had certainly spoken through him, in him. Those who reached this conclusion had themselves prayed the psalms and tasted their fruit; they recognized the savor of God after seeing people grow in prayer thanks to this Book, and to feeling their own hearts burn in the fire of the words . . . These men from among the unknown of the people of Israel saw in Psalms a book marked by the breath of God; they then included it in the canon of the Scriptures. In short, the presence of the Psalms in the Bible is an attestation to the Holy Spirit speaking in David.

To the question we asked as to, who, in the end, speaks in the Book of Psalms, we need to reply, the Holy Spirit.

. . . as Well as the New Testament

We can say this more forcefully given that the New Testament confirms it. Thus, in Acts 1:16, we read: "The Spirit announced by the mouth of David." This formulation could not be clearer; it introduces quotations from the psalms (69:26 and 108:8, cited in Acts 1:20).

The same thing is found in the Letter to the Hebrews, where some verses from Psalm 95 are introduced by the same formula in a more condensed form: "The Holy Spirit said" (Heb 3:7).

Jesus himself spoke in the same vein, but went rather further, adding to what David said: "David spoke in the Holy Spirit" (Mark 12:36). This is an amazing compliment from Jesus, revealing to us finally that the true relation between David and the Spirit is that the Spirit was in David and David in the Spirit.

This relationship is of the same type as that of the Father and the Son: "the Son is in the Father and the Father in the Son" (John 17:21). This relationship evidences a twofold effacement of self, that of David before the Spirit and that of the Spirit before David. In fact, "David is in the Spirit, and the Spirit is in David": a formulation like this is only possible if David effaces himself in favor of the Spirit, and the Spirit likewise in favor of David.

The Humble Holy Spirit

David's effacement of himself is already known to us. We now discover the same quality in the Holy Spirit, a self-effacement which no doubt is still greater, more humble than that of David, since it has hitherto escaped our notice; an effacement so humble that David himself had not fully discerned it until the end of his life in his "last words": "The Spirit of the Lord spoke in me . . . !"

As we looked for the speakers of Psalms, we identified David, men, the Father, the Son . . . but never the Spirit! It needed David to tell us this in the evening of his life, and that other anonymous, humble people with clear spiritual sight tell us too; it needed also to be confirmed by Jesus. If it is so difficult to hear the voice of the Spirit in the Book of Psalms, it is no doubt because he is extremely humble.

The humble Holy Spirit effaces himself discreetly, much more indeed than David!

The humble Holy Spirit speaks through the length of the Book of Psalms, more indeed than any other person, and without letting himself be seen!

The Holy Spirit is the humility of God. He is so humble that he is silence itself. He is so humble that in order to hear him we need to know how to hear the sound of silence . . . (1 Kgs 19:12).

There is no specific psalm which really enables our calloused ears to truly hear the Spirit; nevertheless they all come from him and he speaks in each one! What shall we say to this?

Perhaps we should not seek the Holy Spirit as one particular speaker among others, thereby adding him to the already well-furnished list. The Holy Spirit is rather the one "in whom" the others speak and express themselves, as Jesus rightly tells us. Just as David spoke in[1] the Spirit, the Son speaks in the Spirit, the Father speaks in the Spirit, and we too may be enabled to speak in the Spirit, to pray the psalms in the Spirit.

Nevertheless, he does speak and makes himself heard; David heard him through his own mouth, and both Luke and the author of Hebrews heard him in David's mouth. To hear him it must be necessary to efface ourselves, be silent, listen . . . the more silent we are, the more we are in line to hear him. The more transparent and clean we are, the closer we are to perceiving him. The more humble we are, the more able we are to recognize him.

David functions as a good teacher, effacing himself to leave us to pray. The Holy Spirit leaves his mark as a still better teacher, effacing himself even more as he gives us the gift of prayer. Is it possible for us to have the same relationship with him that he had with David, he in us and we in him? May we, like David, learn this self-effacement in favor of the Spirit?

We were searching for a teacher, and here we have found one who is incomparable, the Holy Spirit! No one knows better how to elucidate what he himself has said through David, of which he is the author. So, if we run up against a phrase in a psalm, a difficulty, we should know to be silent and receive an understanding from him.

---

1. Exactly translating the French; the KJV says David spoke "*by* the Spirit"; many other English translations use "*in*." (Trans.)

This must be the right way to proceed, the correct discipline; if a verse is difficult, we need to listen to it as if hearing it from the very mouth of the Holy Spirit, not from our own, just as we saw to do with regard to the Son. If some word heard as from the Son still seems enigmatic, we need to hear it in the mouth of the Holy Spirit. Why would we wish to appropriate at any price the whole Book of Psalms, and regard each verse of it as an expression of our own prayer? Such a usage is doubtless more a sign of our pride than any humility; this pride can lead us astray and deafen us to the one who is the humility of God. We are to be silent, indeed, to be humbly silent to listen to the Holy Spirit; to be silent and look beyond the one he speaks through, whether the Father, the Son, David . . . or whoever else.

Only the saints are sufficiently humble to be able, through the grace of God, to hear the sound of silence, to hear the Holy Spirit, and to say without the slightest hesitation, "The Holy Spirit has said!" (Heb 3:7). Indeed, the Holy Spirit is the one in whom others express themselves; he is also the one who is heard by those to whom is given the gift of perfectly humble silence. Such was Abba Poemen: "A father asked him one day, 'Who is it that says, As for me I am a companion of all those who fear you?' (Ps 119:63). The elder replied, 'The Holy Spirit says it'" (Apophthegm 710). The father who was questioning Abba Poemen was confronted by the same difficulty as are we. How are we to appropriate and pray a verse in which we are unable to recognize ourselves? Who, indeed, can claim this close bond with all God's faithful? Who would claim to be a friend to all? Abba Poemen was sufficiently enlightened by the Spirit to give the reply: the Holy Spirit says this; he alone is so closely bonded to each of the faithful. Equally, however, it is in the Spirit that we too can make these words our own, as we discover our hearts being enlarged by the Spirit in the communion of the saints.

The Discernment of Spirits . . . _____

If a particular verse is difficult, we must learn to hear it in the mouth of the Holy Spirit and there receive an understanding. This is altogether indispensable, yet we must remember still to be vigilant; another spirit may present itself and explain the verse in its own way, the spirit of evil, Satan, who also proposes a way of interpreting the psalms. How are we to know and discern the difference? How painful to think that we are not like David—in the Spirit and the Spirit in us! We must retain our confidence and ask the Father for the Spirit, just as the Son exhorts: "If you, evil as you are, know how to give good things to your children, how much more will your heavenly Father give the Holy Spirit to those who ask?" (Luke 11:13) Jesus says this immediately following the parable of the importunate friend; we need to ask without letting go, to the point of importuning God!

This request having been made, the Fathers draw our attention to certain signs which will help us discern which spirit is in us. If a number of explanations of the same verse present themselves, hold to the most humble of them, the one which teaches humility, since this comes from the Holy Spirit, who is humility, and not from Satan, for whom humility is impossible; hold to the one which incites love for God and your neighbor, since for Satan this love is impossible; hold to the one which sets God at the center; examine the fruit which is born of your prayer—if prayer of the verse gives birth to joy, peace, gentleness, kindness . . . then it is a work of the Spirit.

. . . as We Listen to the Holy Spirit _____

What if we don't always hear the voice of the Spirit? Then turn your eyes to Christ; turn your attention towards him, to listen to him speak the psalm (if he speaks in the first person), or for you to speak to him, addressing it to him (if he is designated in the second person), or pondering him within the psalm (if he is there in the third person). Then, if your heart begins to burn, the Holy Spirit is in you. What the Holy Spirit says is not in the words, but in the warmth of the words.

We in the Spirit and the Spirit in us; this is what we ask of the Father; that we may know how to pray in the Spirit and that the Spirit come to pray in us. This is to be requested and received, but also learned.

To pray the Book of Psalms in the Spirit means above all learning to be quiet. We have already said this with regard to the Son, but I am saying it again here, this time with regard to the Spirit. Be quiet within a growing humility; the Spirit is humility.

Indeed we must learn to quiet ourselves, to listen to the Spirit, who whispers within the words the Father spoke to Christ: "You are my Son" (Ps 2:7). We must still ourselves ever more deeply and hear the Spirit whisper the response: "Abba, Father" (Rom 8:16–17), and to then marvel as we discover that, in Christ and in the Spirit, the Father says to us too: "You are my son, today have I begotten you!" Such is the depth the Spirit lends to the words of the psalms, equal to the depth of the Father's heart which makes us his children. The energy of love which impels us towards God is a fruit of the Spirit, and it is him we perceive at work when there is warmth in our praise.

We must learn this quietness in order to listen to the Spirit as he enables us to hear Jesus's words from the cross: "My God, my God, why have you forsaken me?" we hear, but also "You have answered me." It is through the Spirit, and in him alone, that we can enter the indefinable encounter of the Father and the Son at the heart of the luminous darkness. We quiet ourselves to allow the Spirit to open our hearts in contemplation.

Then the day comes when the Spirit begins to speak abundantly, and we enter into a profusion of meaning in some word or passage, into a joyous depth in which we ponder the Son, not only on the cross but through all his days, from his birth to the ascension.

This is how it is, for example, with the following verses from Psalm 24. The gates, said to be abased, are invited to lift up their heads[2] to let the king of glory come in; gates which were too abased and blind to recognize, in this king of glory, Christ.

> *Lift up your heads O you gates,*
>
> *Be lifted up, you everlasting doors:*
>
> *Let the king of glory come in.*
>
> *Who is this king of glory?*
>
> *It is the Lord, strong and mighty,*
>
> *The Lord, who is mighty in battle.*

The Spirit enables us to contemplate him as, seated on a donkey, he draws near to the gates of Jerusalem, acclaimed by a crowd waving branches: "Gates, lift up your heads, that the king of glory may enter! Who is this king of whom we are ignorant? It is this very man who approaches in silence, seated on the foal of an ass; he is so humble and so grand, and yet you are depressed and cast down!"

This is how our liturgies invite us to sing this psalm on Palm Sunday, but the Spirit also leads us to ponder this same king as he enters the world through a stable as his gate. The angels had come, not only to alert the shepherds, but also to prepare a cradle: "Gates, lift up your heads . . . But, is it possible that a king would wish to find entrance in a stable? Who can this be? It is the king of the universe; he is no more than a baby, yet this child is so great and you are much too lowly!" This is how, in the Spirit, Irenaeus of Lyon understood the psalm in the second century.

With the author of the Gospel of Nicodemus, the Spirit helps us contemplate the one who stood before the gates of the place of the dead, there to seek his own: "Be lifted up you gates of hell!" "The prince of hell said as though he were ignorant: 'Who is this king of glory?' The Lord strong and mighty, the Lord, mighty in battle, that is who the king of glory is. The Lord looked down from heaven to beneath the

---

2. Literally "'lintels'"; this translation follows the KJV. (Trans.)

earth to hear the cries of those in the fire and deliver the sons of those who were handed over to death . . . The Lord of majesty lightens the eternal darkness."

With Justin Martyr (second century), the Spirit helps us contemplate the one who rose up to heaven, not having any beauty or graciousness of style, his features disfigured by the sufferings of the Passion, so much so that the angels were unable to recognize him: "It is to the angels and powers that the Word of the prophecy was given through the mouth of David, instructing them to lift up the gates that the Lord of all the powers might enter, risen from the dead according to the will of the Father, Jesus Christ." Gregory Nazianzus (fourth century) adds that the doors or gates of heaven were too low "to receive he who was so enlarged by the Passion."

The Spirit thus knocks at the door of our world and our hearts: "Be lifted up you gates and give entrance to the one you still do not know, and who wishes to establish his Kingdom in you." And John Calvin says, commenting on this psalm: "Since the Son of God, having clothed himself with our flesh, has appeared as the king of glory and Lord of hosts, he has not entered into his temple in types or shadows, but really and in fact, that he might live amongst us."

What a symphony the Spirit has composed and conducted across the centuries! Let us be silent, truly silent, until the Spirit has brought us to full wonderment at the symphony that is each verse of these 150 psalms!

Let us be silent as we listen to the Spirit reveal the identity of the true enemy, teaching us not to confuse him with our personal adversaries. Thus the Spirit illumines our spirit to recognize in the "ungodly man" of Psalm 10, none other than Satan, this enemy who still unceasingly seeks to hide himself; but here he is unmasked:

> *The ungodly, in his pride, pursues the poor;*
> *They are taken in the traps he devises.*
> *The ungodly glories in the desire of his own soul,*

The arrogant blasphemes, defying the Lord;

Full of himself, he seeks nothing beyond;

"God is nothing,"—this is his ploy.

All he does always succeeds;

Your decrees are far above him.

He has contempt for all his adversaries.

He says to himself, "Nothing can upset me,

I am far beyond the reach of misfortune."

His cursing mouth is full of fraud and violence,

His tongue lies and wounds.

He sits ready to pounce at the edge of the village

And hides himself to murder the innocent.

With his eyes, he watches for the weak,

He lies in wait like a lion in its den;

He lies in wait to spring upon the poor;

The poor man is seduced, taken in his net.

He crouches and prepares himself;

With all his weight he falls on the feeble . . . [3]

Not once is Satan named in this psalm, but in the Spirit we recognize him.

We are silent, to learn from the Spirit the true nature of the spiritual battle to which the Book of Psalms invites us.

We are silent, to allow the Spirit to rise up in our hearts to purify us with the words of pure prayer, the words of true innocence, the words of true repentance, of true compassion, of genuine intercession and adoration . . .

The Spirit takes us still further; he leads us and inducts us into the history of Israel, to experience the exodus from Egypt and the crossing of the Jordan (Psalm 114), the fall of Jerusalem (Psalm 74), the exile

3. There are many variations across translations of this psalm; this follows the author's French (Trans.).

(Psalm 137), the return from exile (Psalm 126) . . . In the Spirit we are not just spectators of these events but we live them in the communion of the saints.

The Spirit leads us again, making us witnesses of the creation of the world, leading us to contemplate, in Psalm 104, what no one has ever seen. Who other than the one who "hovered over the waters" could enable us to contemplate the first dawn of the world?

The Spirit makes us advance witnesses of the last judgment, and puts onto our lips Psalm 82: "In the divine assembly, God presides; with the gods all around, he judges . . ."

It is the Spirit again who leads us, beyond the first or last day, into the eternal praise of the seraphim and enables us to hear the Trisagion[4] and its harmonies! "Holy, holy, holy," cry the seraphim (Isa 6:3), in eternal praise (Rev 4:8). Psalm 99 is an echo of this with its threefold chant of "he is holy," in verse 3, then in verse 5 and finally verse 9, and all the harmonies in between. In this way the Holy Spirit gives us entry into the depths of cosmic praise.

In short, the Spirit takes us into true prayer, the pure prayer to which we aspire, for which we sought a master, one through whom God himself is present to guide us. The Father has given us the words of prayer and the Son has come to pray with us; and here the Spirit comes to pray within us, a triple mobilization of the Trinitarian God in our favor. How could God do more?

The Spirit Sounds the Depths of God

With the Holy Spirit we reach the final depths of the Book of Psalms and of prayer.

It is in the Spirit that David speaks of the Father and of the Son, as Jesus says in Mark 12:35: "The Lord said to my Lord . . ." It is also

---

4. The Trisagion (Thrice Holy), a standard liturgical hymn or chant in Eastern churches. (Trans.)

in the Spirit that David speaks of the Son to the Father: "Who is the Son of Man that you should care for him?" (Ps 8:4) and "Look upon the face of your Messiah" (Ps 84:9). It is also in the Spirit again that he speaks of the Father to the Son: "God, your God, has anointed you with the oil of gladness" (Ps 45:7).

All these verses immerse us in the mystery of the Trinity: in the Spirit . . . the Father . . . the Son . . . But the Book of Psalms has still more to reveal as David effaces himself entirely to leave us alone with the Trinity. It is in the Spirit that the Son speaks to the Father, and in the Spirit that we hear the Son say to the Father: "My God, my God, why have you forsaken me?" together with "you have answered me. . ." It is also in the Spirit that the Father says to the Son, and in the Spirit that we hear it: "You are my Son; today have I begotten you" (Ps 2:7) . . .

In the same way, in the Spirit, we enter into the mystery of the intimacy between the Father and the Son, the mystery of the heart of God. This is the real depth of the Psalms, the depth of the Trinity; it is a profundity the Spirit reveals to us, and which bestows on the Psalter its profound unity, proceeding as it does from the God who is one; it is a profundity beyond our reach but which envelops us. It is also a profundity which is confessed and celebrated by the whole of the monastic tradition when it concludes each psalm with a Trinitarian doxology in order to glorify the true source, the true light.

In the Book of Psalms we are brought into the prayer of the Son, alongside that of the Spirit; but there remains a final prayer for us to uncover, that of the Father; this is prayer most discreetly expressed, which the Spirit, again, enables us to hear.

Thus, in Psalm 2:7, the Father addresses the Son and declares to him: "You are my Son, today have I begotten you." He then makes a request of him in prayer, in the fullness of his love: "Ask of me and I will give you the nations for an inheritance." Here, indeed, the Father prays the Son, "ask of me, I pray . . ."

We find the same thing in Psalm 110, where, when "the Lord said to my Lord," the Father says to the Son, "Take your seat at my right hand, and I will make your enemies the footstool of your throne." "Take your seat": this invitation is a true prayer, a marvelous prayer, full of love, in which the Father honors the Son.

The Son prays, the Holy Spirit prays, and now the Father himself prays too. The Holy Trinity is prayer; God is prayer. The Book of Psalms leads us into this great mystery; it conducts us right into the depths of the praying heart of God. God's very being is prayer!

To pray the Book of Psalms is to enter into God's prayer; it is to enter into the being of God, who is prayer. We enter the Trinitarian mystery of God, not through our own will but because the Trinity takes hold of us, surrounds us, leads us, making his own sanctuary within us, his place of rest. We enter into the Trinity because the Trinity enters into us; the Trinity in us and ourselves in the Trinity in an eternal, mutual effacement . . .

I have no words to take us further into such a great mystery . . . We can only be silent and adore.

Prayer is the splendor of God, a splendid beauty whose source is the Father, a splendor we contemplate in the Son, and is given us to contemplate by the Spirit.

Prayer is the splendor of God; the person who prays is fashioned and transfigured into the image of God. It us thus that prayer is the splendor of human beings.

We all, with unveiled face, gaze into and reflect as in a mirror the glory of the Lord, and are transformed into the same likeness, from glory to glory, as by the Lord, the Spirit. (2 Cor 3:18)

CHAPTER 5

God Is Listening for the 151ˢᵗ Psalm

OUR INITIAL QUESTION WAS, Who will teach us to pray? The first response was that God himself comes to teach us. Then we became more precise in our answer: this God who comes to teach us to pray is the Trinitarian God, whose very being is prayer since each of the three persons prays.

The Father teaches by providing the Book of Psalms as his very own prayer, which he then proposes become ours. These words trace out the way to God's heart and describe it as a pathway of love.

The Son teaches us to pray by praying the psalms alongside us, with us, before us, for us; he teaches by living out his prayer before the Father, all the way to the cross, where he is the embodiment of prayer.

The Holy Spirit teaches us to pray by praying the psalms in us in the shadow of the cross, where he reveals the profundity of the psalms and of the divine mystery.

There is no teacher greater than this, the Trinitarian teacher, the source of prayer, the way of prayer and the goal of prayer; a teacher whose very being is prayer. In the Book of Psalms he envelops us, takes hold of us and fashions us, forming us into his image, into a being of prayer. In Psalms, we discover this teacher, listen to him and ponder him.

Our initial question concerned prayer and our ignorance of God; this being so great, we asked, aren't we sure to be mistaken as to whom we are praying to and so go far astray when we pray? Surely not, since, as he teaches us to pray, God introduces us to God! In his prayer, the Father makes the Son known to us; in his prayer, the Son makes the Father known to us; and there is no one who knows the depths of the heart of God apart from the Spirit who teaches us by praying within us. Who knows the Son beside his begetter? Who knows the Spirit beside the one from whom he proceeds? Thus led by God, we have no better teacher to bring us to God.

Still further, the initial question was this: do I really know myself sufficiently, so that my prayer may truly reflect my inmost being? In Psalms we find that God reveals us to ourselves in our true depths: "You are my Son, today I have begotten you," a truth that becomes clear on the cross. Nobody knows us better than the one who created us, who fashions us anew in his image and sounds the depths of our heart to cause pure prayer to gush forth as from a sanctuary.

> *You search me, Lord, and you know;*
>
> *You know when I sit down and when I rise.*
>
> *From far away you penetrate my thoughts . . .*
>
> *It is you who formed my kidneys,*
>
> *Who knit me together in my mother's womb . . .*
>
> *My bones were not hidden from you*
>
> *When I was fashioned in secret,*
>
> *Formed in the bowels of the earth . . .* (Psalm 139)

Nothing of myself that escapes my understanding can escape God; nothing unknown to me is unknown to him. By his Spirit he illuminates me as to myself and makes of the Book of Psalms a reflection of my true being.

Our initial question had also to do with God's silence, sometimes so weighty as to be difficult to bear; but here in the Book of Psalms we are ourselves invited to silence, to hear, rising out of the silence, the prayer of the Son, the prayer of the Spirit and even the prayer of the Father. Then the silence becomes love, in which our prayer finds its place.

87

Our initial question also concerned the words of prayer: what are the words which find their way to God's heart? In the psalms, God himself provides such words; he speaks them with us and in us, making of us beings of prayer, in his image.

We have seen how important it is to learn to be quiet, the better to pray; the apprenticeship of prayer is conducted above all in silence. We maintain silence through 150 psalms in order to listen to the Son pray to the Father in the Spirit. We are silent to listen to the Spirit pray to the Father in contemplation of the Son. We are silent to listen to the Father pray to the Son in the Spirit. We are silent that we may be fashioned by the prayer of God, and become in turn beings of prayer. We are also silent in order to listen to the people of God pray with the angels and the archangels in the communion of the saints. We are silent so that we may enter into this prayer and add to it our own. We are silent, again, to listen to the breath of the entire creation; to hear day speak to day and night to night (Ps 19:2–3); to hear the young of the raven calling upon God for its sustenance (Ps 147:9); to hear the snow and the mist, the sun and the moon sing of God's grandeur (Ps 148:3, 8), and all the cries of the earth taking form in the psalms.

Then, after such silence, our prayer will be strong and deep and dense, shot through with love, humility, compassion and tenderness.

The art of prayer perhaps consists quite simply in knowing how to enter into the psalms, or, more exactly, to allow the psalms to enter into us, opening us up to the prayer which God wishes to birth within us, opening our impure hearts to the pure prayer which comes to purify. The art of prayer is to open ourselves to God in a readiness to marvel at how God himself opens us towards himself; everything we believe to be our own effort comes from him. The art of prayer has Psalms as its studio and God as its craftsman, a craftsman who works in us in his grace. God opens us to himself, giving birth to our prayer, praying in us.

When the craftsman draws near and shapes our lives, the evidence of his passing is the praise that he births, evidence never before found in human hearts; prayer full of love which vibrates with the reflection of his beauty; the evidence of God's approach is the splendor it brings us. Such is the Book of Psalms which is given us, a studio of prayer where God stands to behold his work, a school of prayer with 150 entrances. One last question now springs forth: what of our personal prayer, that prayer profoundly our own which leaps from our heart, that prayer in which we can speak to God in our own words of our joys and our pains, our thirst and our love? What place has our poor prayer beside these 150 treasures?

Our personal prayer is that before which God guards the deepest silence, to which he listens with infinite attention. Our personal prayer is Psalm 151! In this prayer, God contemplates the splendor which is ours; in it he recognizes the fruit of his grace.